Admin's Guide

CentOS

Version 7

Shiv Kumar Goyal

Preface

This book is for system administrators or Linux enthusiast. This book is written keeping in mind practical aspects of CentOS Linux. I will call this book as no non-sense book. If you are plaining to deploy CentOS Linux or you are maintaining CentOS machine than this book is for you. All procedures written in the book are to the point with available screen shots and output samples This book leaves no stone unturned to cover all practical parts of Linux administration. If you are short of time and hates reading bulky books, then this book is for you it covers all articles from basics to advance level.

I hope you will like this book

Thanks

Shiv Kumar Goyal

Table of Contents

Chapter 1.

Introduction

An operating system is piece of software, which manages hardware resources on your computer. OS is a layer that runs in between your applications and hardware. To run any application, you require operating system on your machine. There are lot of operating system available in the market like MS windows, Apple Mac OS, Unix, Linux etc. Just like Windows 7, MS Windows 10 and Mac OS, Linux is an operating system. Linux is open source operating system that means source code is freely available. The benefit of open source is that anyone can see the source code and modify it if required.

In 1991 Linus Torvalds started Linux project. Linux was originally developed for Intel based personal computers but eventually it had been ported on other platforms also. Not only on PC, Linux kernel is also used in Android Operating system on your smartphones. As Linux is open source project lot of companies and individual used this source code and started creating own Linux distributions. Today there are thousands of Linux distributions in the market, but there are some distribution that enjoy major chunk of share among Linux users. Over the time lot of Linux communities and companies use these popular distributions to create their own distribution flavor by modifying or adding some packages. Broadly, we can classify Linux distribution based on their source distribution for example CentOS, Oracle and Scientific Linux are based on Redhat whereas Debian based distributions are Ubuntu, Mint, tails and PureOS etc.

Free V/s Paid

Linux although is open source project but there are two types of Linux distribution available one is free and other is paid. Free is self-explanatory you do not have to pay anything. If you have any problem, you can take help of volunteers working for that Linux community. However, problem is that this type of support is not time bond as it is voluntarily. For corporate sector where Linux is used in production environment, it is a big problem. So companies who uses mission critical Linux servers and computers prefers paid type of Linux Distribution where they pay fixed amount as subscription and support fee to get services with SLA. These paid Linux distribution companies keeps team of Linux experts to provide support and fixes.

The prominent players in free Linux are Ubuntu, Debian, Fedora, CentOS, Opensuse etc. Red hat and SUSE are major players in non-free enterprise Linux distribution.

CentOS and Red hat Linux

Red Hat Enterprise Linux is known for its stability. As name suggest it is enterprise level Linux. The CentOS (short for **C**ommunity **ENT**erprise **O**perating **S**ystem) Linux distribution is free Linux distribution derived from source code of Red hat Enterprise Linux. It is enterprise class Linux distribution. Unlike Red Hat where you have to pay subscription fee for updates and upgrades, CentOS is fully free. CentOS Linux provides same software packages as Red hat but without support from Red hat. CentOS takes source code from Red Hat repositories. Using this source code CentOS rebrand it after removing Red Hat logos, trademarks and proprietary software. CentOS also removes and modify some original software provided by Red Hat like subscription manager, which is not required in CentOS.

Chapter 2.

New Features in CentOS Linux Version 7

CentOS Linux distribution is a stable platform derived from the sources of Red Hat Enterprise Linux (RHEL). With new version 7, CentOS has brought many improvements from its previous versions. Here is a summary of new features came with CentOS version 7:-

- New installation GUI.
- Automatic partitioning with more choices like LVM, BRTFS and standard partitioning.
- LVM Cache provides option to use small fast block device such as SSD as cache device for large slower block device.
- Parallel NFS pNFS is part of NFSv4.1 standard that allows clients access storage devices directly and in parallel.
- XFS file system.
- Kernel version 3.10
- Dynamic kernel patching which empowers you to patch the kernel without rebooting.
- Swap memory compression.
- Non uniform memory access NUMA.
- Hardware Error Reporting Mechanism.
- Linux containers with Docker format.
- **Systemd** is system and service manager for Linux and replaces SysV and upstart.
- Support for 7th-generation Core i3, i5, and i7 Intel processors.
- Nested virtualization with KVM.

- New **firewalld** dynamic firewall daemon.
- New **Gnome 3** Desktop.
- ABRT - Automatic Bug Reporting Tool
- GRUB 2.

## Chapter 3

Minimum system requirement

Following are minimum requirement to install CentOS Version 7. However, it is ideal to have more resources than this for optimum performance of your machine

Processor   1GHz or faster

System memory (RAM)   1GB

Hard disk   10GB

Graphical installation of CentOS requires a minimum screen resolution of 800x600. If you have device with lower resolution you should do VNC installation.

GNOME3 is the default desktop environment for CentOS version 7. However, you can also install other desktop environment of your choice like KDE, Mate, LXDE, LXQt .

Chapter 4.

Installation

In this chapter we will covers installation of CentOS Linux version 7. The installation of CentOS is very easy and straightforward. This chapter is designed in such way even if you do not have prior knowledge of Linux you can install CentOS easily as whole installation is explained step by step with screenshots.

Installation of CentOS includes following steps

1. Download Media Image

You can download the image directly if internet connection is stable otherwise you can download using torrent client.

2. Verify image

Once you finish downloading of installation image, it is good practice to verify the integrity of the downloaded image.

3. Write image to media

Once you finish downloading of installation image, it is good practice to verify the integrity of the downloaded image.

4. Select way, how you want install it .There are two common ways to install:-

1. Interactive

Interactive method is normal installation method, which can be either Text based or GUI. This method of installation requires user interaction for inputs during installation.

2. Automated using Kickstart

For Kickstart installation, we have to create a single file containing answers to all the questions CentOS installation normally asks during interactive installation. Once the installation starts, no user intervention is required.

5. Verify the installation.

Interactive installation

In the last section, we summarized the steps involved in the installation. In this section we will go through these steps thoroughly.

Download Media Image

First thing first, for installation we require media. For media preparation, you have to download the installation ISO image. There are two ways to do that:-

1. Download ISO image directly from the site.
2. Use torrent client to download ISO, in case you have unstable internet connection

Open the internet explorer on your MS windows machine. Open the site of CentOS https://www.centos.org/

Press Download button it will bring next page. Here for direct download press **DVD ISO** and for torrent download press **via Torrent**.

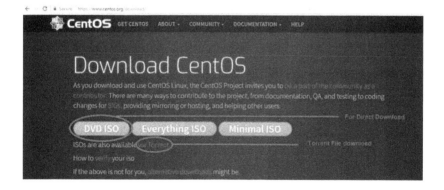

If you press DVD ISO. It will bring the screen to select the mirror for download. Select any link near to your place. It will start downloading ISO image.

If you press via Torrent, it will bring screen to select the mirror.

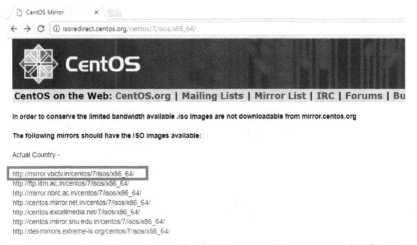

Once you select the mirror, it will bring another screen for file selection. From this screen, select file of few KBs size.

Index of /centos/7/isos/x86_64

Name	Last modified	Size	Description
Parent Directory	-		
0_README.txt	2017-09-13 20:30	2.4K	
CentOS-7-x86_64-DVD-..>	2017-09-06 16:29	4.2G	
CentOS-7-x86_64-DVD-..>	2017-09-13 20:08	169K	
CentOS-7-x86_64-Ever..>	2017-09-06 16:29	8.1G	
CentOS-7-x86_64-Ever..>	2017-09-13 20:09	324K	
CentOS-7-x86_64-Live..>	2017-09-05 20:52	1.2G	
CentOS-7-x86_64-Live..>	2017-09-13 20:09	49K	
CentOS-7-x86_64-Live..>	2017-09-05 21:02	1.7G	
CentOS-7-x86_64-Live..>	2017-09-13 20:09	67K	

After downloading this torrent file, add this file to torrent client. You can use any torrent client like uTorrent, bit torrent etc.

Preparing Media

Once file has been downloaded, check the integrity of file. If you have downloaded file on MS Windows computer you can download free File Checksum Integrity Verifier tool from site

https://raylin.wordpress.com/downloads/md5-sha-1-checksum-utility/

Run this utility, select downloaded ISO image file, select sha256. Now open **sha256sum.txt** file. This file is available on the same site from where you had downloaded torrent file. Copy the sha256sum from that file in Hash textbox and press verify.

Write image to media

After verification of image, you can write the ISO file to DVD. If DVD Drive in your computer is not working or not present you can write this image to USB flash drive. The procedure to write image to USB flash drive is given bellow:-

Creating USB Media on Windows

1. Download media writer from

https://github.com/MartinBriza/MediaWriter/releases

2. Double click the downloaded file to install it and follow the Wizard.

3. Once installation is finished run **Fedora Media Writer** from start menu.

4. Once Fedora image writer is running, from the menu select Custom image.

5. Select ISO image file and plug the USB flash media. Once it is ready press Write.

6. Now USB flash is ready for installation.

Steps to do installation

Booting with Media

Once media is ready. Make media as first boot device in the BOIS of computer. Check the manual of your computer to change boot priority. Once system boots, it will show Installation menu, Select **Install CentOS Linux 7**

Select Language and press **Continue**

14

This will bring **Installation Summary** Screen.

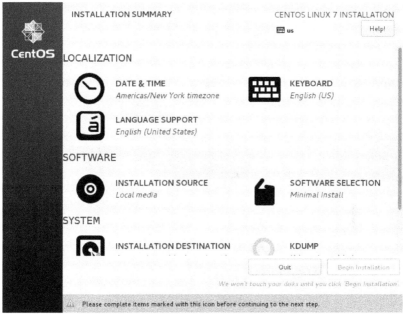

Select **Date and time** to modify date time and time zone.

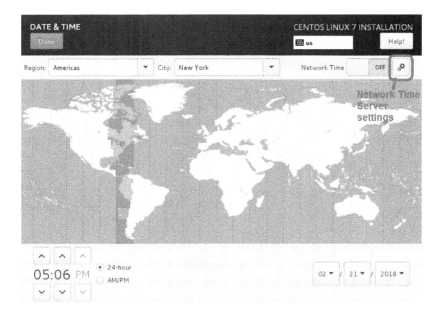

If you are using Network Time server for time synchronization you can configure it here. To use network time, change the position of **Network time** button to **on** position and press small gear button for network time server settings. Once you enter the server settings press **Done**.

On the next screen, If required select and change the Keyboard layout. To add new keyboard press **+** sign and to remove existing keyboard press **–** sign

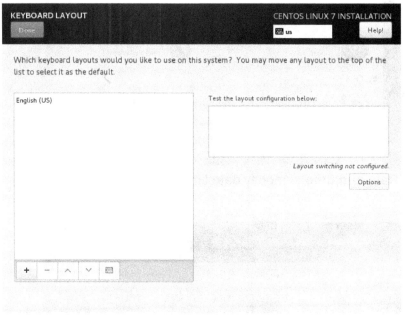

Click **Software Selection** from **Installation summary** screen and select required **Base environment**. For demo purpose I selected **Server with GUI**.

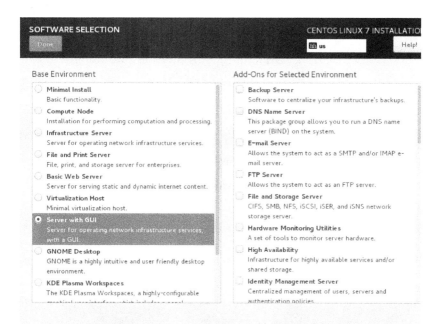

On Installation Summary screen if you scroll down you will see more options, select **Installation Destination**.

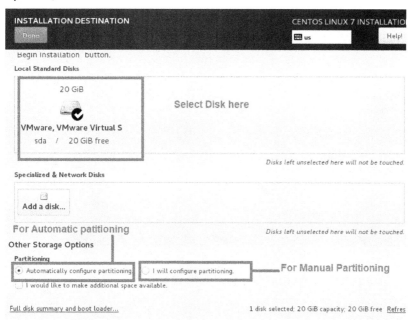

Either leave it to **Automatic Configure partitioning** or you can select **I will configure partitioning** for manual partitioning.

In case you select Manual partitioning, you have to add minimum two partition in case for standard partitioning and three in case of BTRFS partitioning. The partitions are **boot**, **/** (root) and **swap**. Boot should be at least 500MB, root should at least 10GB and swap partition should be equal to or more than physical RAM in the system. You write the capacity in human readable format like 10G for 10GB and 500M for 500MB.

Now Click **Network and Host Name** for configuring network settings and hostname.

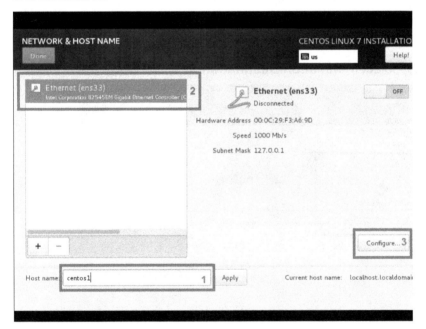

1. In **Host Name** textbox write the hostname.
2. Select the network card
3. Press configure button.

As you press, Configure button it will bring network configuration screen.

1. Select IPv4 setting tab
2. Select method as manual from drop down menu if you have static IP address otherwise leave it Automatic.
3. In case of static IP address, press Add button
   1. Write IP address, Netmask and gateway
   2. DNS server.

Select General Tab and select **Automatically connect to this network when it is available.** Otherwise after booting network will not be connected. Press **Save** to save setting and press **Done** on **Network and Hostname.**

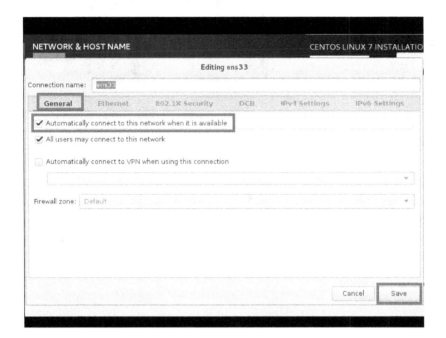

Press **Begin installation**. It will bring screen on which it will show progress of installation, option to set root password and create one new users.

Select **Root password** and set root password.

During installation, you have to create one normal user. Click **Create New** user. Provide Full name of the user, username and password and press done

Once copping is finished **Reboot**.

When System Restarts it will bring License information. Select **I accept the license agreement** and press Done.

Now press **Finish Installation**.

Now you have finished your installation. It's time to connect to the newly created server from remote machine, we will discuss how to connect your windows machine in next chapter.

## Chapter 5

Connecting Your PC to CentOS Server

In practical life you occasionally work on server, usually you connect from your PC and do administration. You may be using MS windows 7 or MS windows 10 on your PC. First thing you require to connect to Linux host is a software. There are many options like VanDyke, bitvise and putty. Among them PuTTY is free and very popular option.

PuTTY is an SSH and telnet client, developed originally by Simon Tatham for the Windows platform. It is a software that gives text terminal access of server on remote MS Windows machine. To install putty open internet explorer and download putty from

http://www.chiark.greenend.org.uk/~sgtatham/putty/latest.html

Once you have downloaded the putty install it.

When you start putty you will see following screen. On this screen

1. Write the IP Address of the newly installed server.

2. Select the Protocol as **SSH**

3. Give name of Session like Centos1 or linux1 etc

4. Press **Save** button

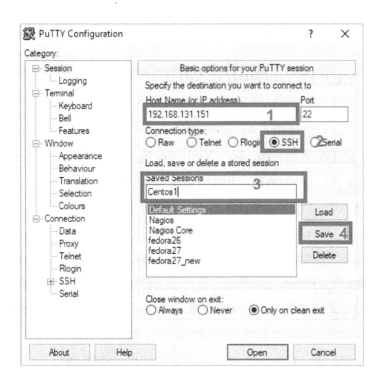

Once session is saved either double click the session name to connect to the Linux host or select the session press **Load** then press **Open**

## Chapter 6

Network

Network is group of two or more computers connected together. Network allows interconnection between different machines. You require network card on each computer to connect. Every network card has physical address known as **M**edia **A**ccess **C**ontrol address (MAC address). MAC address works on layer 2 of OSI model. Manufacturer of network interface card assigns MAC addresses to network cards. As network card can go faulty and needs replacement, with replacement of network card the MAC address will change. To overcome this problem we assign IP address to network card, which works on layer 3 of OSI model. As IP address are still numeric value it is difficult to remember, more over there is possibility of IP address may change in case of dynamic IPs. To make life easy for humans we use **hostname,** which nothing but name of computers.

Just to give an idea about OSI model and list of applications and devices with their respective layers, a chart is given bellow.

Seven layer of OSI and TCP Mapping

OSI Model	TCP Model	Application	Address	Devices
7:Application layer	Application Layer	HTTP / Telnet / SSH	Applications DNS, DHCP.ntp,HTTP,	
6:Presentation layer		SSL / MIME		
5: Session layer		Sockets and Remote Procedure Call (RPC)		
4: Transport layer	Transport layer	Transmission Control Protocol (TCP)	TCP/UDP	Gateway
3: Network layer	Internet layer	Internet Protocol (IP)	IP4, IP6, IPX, ICMP	Router, firewall Layer 3 switch
2: Data link layer	Network Access Layer	Ethernet / Frame Relay	MAC address, ARP	Bridge Layer 2 switch
1: Physical layer		IEEE 802.x	Ethernet	HUB

Commands to check network configuration

After fresh installation, it is good idea to check the network configuration. As a best practice note down this configuration

Show IP address

```
# ip addr show
```

Or

```
# ifconfig -a
```

Show Link status

```
# ip link show
```

Show routing table

```
# ip route
```

Or

```
# netstat -rn
```

Check and change hostname

Show hostname

```
# hostname
```

Change hostname

Whenever you want to change hostname, you have to change it in two steps

1. Change hostname using command **hostnamectl**
2. Next change entry in /etc/hosts

1. Give hostnamectl command status to check the current

```
# hostnamectl status
   Static hostname: centos1
         Icon name: computer
           Chassis: n/a
        Machine ID: 98c0429d893c48b88fba101f95aa70ca
           Boot ID: 864f0f4e99cd4442b4f388a15a7fc132
```

Or

```
# hostname
```

2. Change the hostname

```
# hostnamectl set-hostname centos2
```

3. Next step is to change **/etc/hosts** file

```
127.0.0.1 centos2 localhost.localdomain localhost
```

Setting Up the DNS Name Resolution

Whenever you write hostname instead of IP address to ping or to connect Linux host. You have multiple option to resolve hostname to IP address.

- Local file i.e. /etc/hosts
- DNS server
- NIS

/etc/hosts

/etc/hosts is file which stores hostname to IP address mapping. It provides ability to resolve hostname without using DNS server. We generally use this file if we are connecting to limited number of host due scope or security reason.

Format

IP_address   hostname aliases

Example

```
127.0.0.1                    centos1 localhost
::1                          centos1 localhost
```

```
192.168.228.129          centos1
```

DNS

/etc/resolv.conf

/etc/resolv.conf is required in case DNS is used to resolve host names. You need to put your DNS server IP addresses in this file. Generally, you need one name server, but you can include up to three if you want redundancy. If the first one on the list is not responding, system tries to resolve against the next one on the list, and so on.

Edit **/etc/resolv.conf** to add list of name servers, like this:

```
nameserver 8.8.8.8
nameserver 8.8.8.9
nameserver 1.2.3.6
```

Changing order for hostname resolution

/etc/nsswitch.conf

If hosts file and DNS configuration is there in **resolv.conf** in your server, Whenever you do hostname resolution the system looks for local file **(/etc/hosts)** for entry of hostname and respective IP address. If there is no entry, it looks for **/etc/resolv.conf** file for DNS configuration. If there is no DNS configuration also then it will check for NIS configuration. However, you can change this behavior by changing order in **/etc/nsswitch.conf** file.

```
vi /etc/nsswitch.conf
```

```
#hosts:     db files nisplus nis dns
hosts:      files dns
```

In this example search sequence is first files means **/etc/hosts** then DNS server.

Modifying Network configuration

In the earlier versions of CentOS, Network configuration was handled using files. However, in the recent version of CentOS it uses network manager. Network manager is dynamic network configuration and control daemon. It manages network devices and connections. The ifcfg configuration files which were used traditionally, still supported in CentOS.

Network Manager configures

1. IP address
2. Static routes
3. Network aliases
4. VPN configuration
5. DNS information

Check the status of networkmanager daemon

```
# systemctl status NetworkManager
```

Start Networkmanager if it is not working

```
# systemctl start NetworkManager
```

Enable it to start automatically with system start (Most of the time it is not requires as networkmanager is configured by default to start automatically)

```
# systemctl enable NetworkManager
```

Changing IP Address using Graphical interface

If static IP address is configured in your system or want to change dynamic IP to static IP address following steps are there

6. Login as root

7. Click network manager icon and select Wired settings

8. Select click setting icon is small gear icon

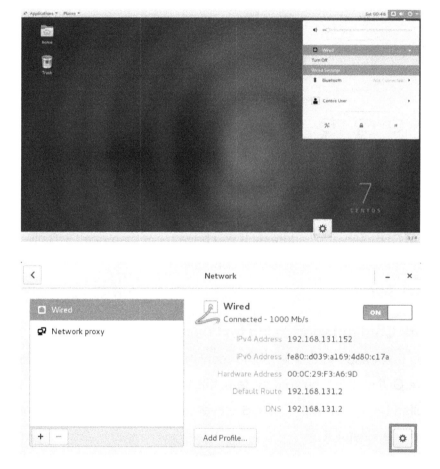

9. Select IPv4 settings

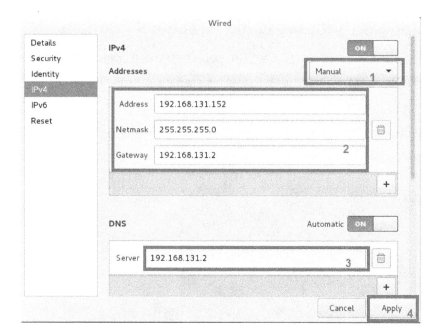

1. Select **Manual** from IPv4 Method
2. Give IP address, Netmask and Gateway
3. Write DNS server IP address. If you have more than one DNS give all IP addresses separated with commas
4. Press **Apply**

Network Configuration using text based interface nmtui

Nmtui is text based interface tool for configuring networking. If you do not have GUI installed on your system, this tool is very helpful. This tool is installed by default with CentOS server installation. In case it is not there you can install it

```
# yum install NetworkManager-tui
```

To start nmtui

```
# nmtui
```

Commands

Edit the connection setting

Syntax

```
nmtui edit connection_name
```

Example

```
# nmtui edit ens33
```

Connect the disconnected connection

Syntax

```
nmtui connect connection_name
```

Example

```
# nmtui connect ens33
```

Change hostname using nmtui

Syntax

```
nmtui hostname new_hostname
```

Example

```
# nmtui hostname centos2
```

Modifying IP address using NMTUI

Start nmtui

```
# nmtui
```

1. Select **Edit a connection**

2. Select the connection profile from the list and press **Edit**

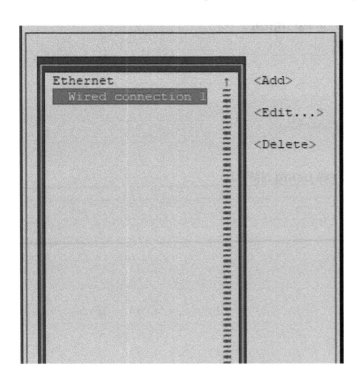

3. From the next screen press SPACE BAR key on IPv4 configuration to get popup menu. Select **Manual** to set static IP address.

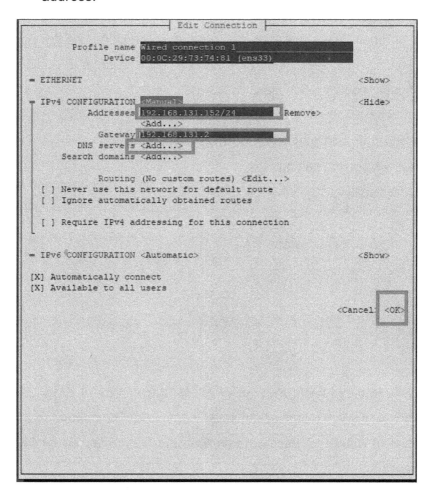

4. Give IP Address with Netmask in next column.

5. Write gateway and DNS in respective fields and press **OK**

6. Press ESC key to come out from NMTUI

Modifying network configuration using configuration files

If you do not have Graphical desktop and you love to work on configuration files, you can still use configuration files to control networking. In this example, I will explain how to change IP address of host using configuration files.

Changing IP address using configuration files

1. Check current setting

```
# ip addr show
```

2. Check current devices

```
[root@centos2]# nmcli d
DEVICE   TYPE       STATE       CONNECTION
ens33    ethernet   connected   ens33
lo       loopback   unmanaged   --
```

3. Edit **/etc/sysconfig/network-scripts/ifcfg-***. Where **ifcfg-*** file is device file you just checked in last command. The command output shows **ens33** as device name then the file name will be **ifcfg-ens33**

```
# vi /etc/sysconfig/network-scripts/ifcfg-ens33
```

4. Change **/etc/sysconfig/network-scripts/ifcfg-ens33** file depending on whether you have static IP address or you are using DHCP

Static	DHCP
DEVICE=ens33	DEVICE=ens33
BOOTPROTO=static	BOOTPROTO=dhcp
IPADDR =192.168.0.132	
NETMASK=255.255.255.0	
GATEWAY=192.168.0.1	
ONBOOT=yes	

5. Restart network services

```
# systemctl restart network
```

Adding static route using configuration file

To change static routes or to add new routes do the following

1. Check current routing table

```
# netstat -rn
```

    or

```
# route -n
```

    or

```
# ip route show
```

2. Edit **/etc/sysconfig/network-scripts/route-interfacefile** and add X.X.X.X/X via Y.Y.Y.Y dev interface Where X.X.X.X is IP address or network and Y.Y.Y.Y is gateway used by X.X.X.X

```
# vi /etc/sysconfig/network-scripts/route-ens33
```

Example

```
10.0.0.0/8 via 192.168.1.1
```

3. Restart network services

```
# systemctl restart network
```

4. Check the routing table again

```
# route -n
```

5. Ping the destination address

```
# ping 10.0.0.2
```

Changing DNS server using configuration file

Edit **/etc/resolv.conf**

```
search example.com        // give own FQDN
nameserver 8.8.8.8        // IPaddress of first DNS
nameserver 8.8.4.4        // IPaddress of Second DNS
```

Managing network interface

Bring down Ethernet interface

Syntax

Ifdown interface_name

Example

```
# ifdown ens33
```

Bring up Ethernet interface

Syntax

Ifup interface_name

Example

```
# ifup ens33
```

Important Network Commands

Task	Command
Check connectivity between two systems	ping *IP_address of other system* Example ping 10.1.1.2
Check IP address configuration	ifconfig -a or ip addr show
Check configuration of network card	cat /etc/sysconfig/network-scripts/ifcfg-*
Check routing table	ip route show
Querying DNS	dig
Local file to resolve hosts to IP address	/etc/hosts
DNS server configuration file	/etc/resolv.conf

## Chapter 7

Users Management

If you are not the only user of the computer and others are also using it. For security and privacy purpose, it is recommended to create separate username for each user so that every user can keep his data in their respective home folder. The control of users and groups is a central part of system administration.

User and group

A **user** is anyone who uses a computer. Users on Linux machine are ether people or accounts. The users are further logically grouped together in **groups**. Group is logical entity to organize users together based on their properties. It can be either same department, same place or same work.

Root user V/S normal user

In CentOS Linux root is the default administrator of the system. Root is most powerful user among all users on CentOS server. Once you login as root, you can do anything on the server. Unlike normal user root user can read write and modify the files and directories of all other users. **root** user can even modify and delete system files also. Hence, it is absolutely important to keep the root user's password in safe custody.

Login as root user on graphical terminal

If Graphical desktop environment is installed, after system boot you will get login screen.

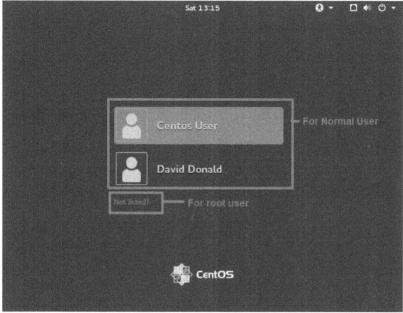

You can press the user's icon to login as normal user. To login as root user, you select **Not listed?** from the graphical login screen.

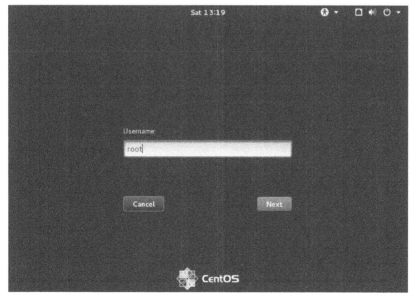

Once text box for login name appears type **root** and press **Enter**, type the root's password that you selected during installation at the password prompt, and press **Enter**.

User Management using GUI

To create user in CentOS.

1. Login as root user.

2. Click **Applications** from panel click **Setting** under **System tools.** It will open **All Setting** window.

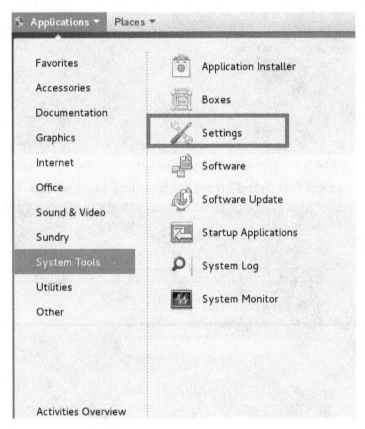

3. In **All settings window** under **System** category click **Users.**

4. It will bring users group management dialog button

5. To add user press + button. It will bring another dialog box with following fields

   Account Type: You have two options Standard or administrator

   Full Name   : Type Full name of the user

   Username   : Type username of user you want to create

   Allow User to set password when they next login/Set a password now : There are two ways to set password. First way, you can force user to set password on next login. Other way is by setting temporary password by administrator so that new user can change password at his convenience. This way you add additional security layer so that no unauthorized user can use newly created username before user sets password.

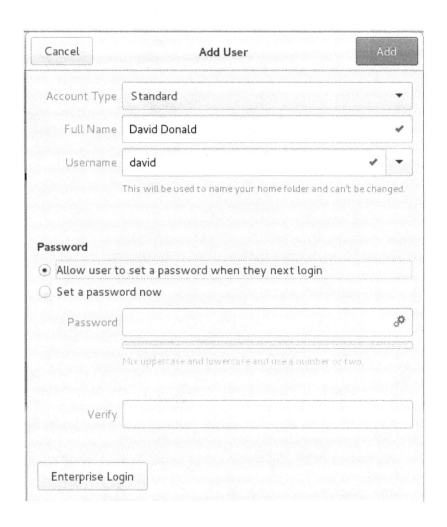

Users and Group management using Command Line

User management using command line is very interesting and it offers more options and flexibility.

Add User

Syntax

```
# useradd -c "Full name of user" username
```

Example

```
# useradd -c "Adam mark" adam1
```

Now set the password

Syntax

```
# passwd username
```

Example

```
# passwd  adam1
```

Modify user

Syntax

```
# usermod option username
```

Example

```
# usermod -c "Adam markwell" adam1
```

Delete/remove user

Syntax

```
# userdel username
```

Example

```
# userdel adam1
```

Display information about user

Show current user's information

Syntax

```
$ id
```

Example

```
$ id
```

Show information of other users

Syntax

```
# id username
```

Example

```
# id adam1
```

Change password for other user

Syntax

```
# passwd username
```

Example

```
# passwd adam1
```

Change own password

```
$ passwd
```

List password expiry information

Synatx

```
# chage -l username
```

Example

```
# chage -l adam1
```

Set password expiry

root user can set the password expiry date for any user. In this example password will expire after 10 from last password change.

Syntax

```
# chage -M no of days from last password change usename
```

Example

```
# chage -l adam1
Last password change                          : Feb 25,
2018
Password expires                              :
never
Password inactive                             :
never
Account expires                               :
never
Minimum number of days between password change    : 0
Maximum number of days between password change    :
99999
Number of days of warning before password expires : 7


# chage -M 10  adam1
# chage -l adam1
Last password change                          : Feb 25,
2018
Password expires                              : Mar 07,
2018
Password inactive                             :
never
Account expires                               :
never
Minimum number of days between password change    : 0
Maximum number of days between password change    : 10
Number of days of warning before password expires : 7
```

Note –M option will update both "Password expires" and "Maximum number of days between password change"

Disable password expiration for user

Syntax

```
# chage -I -1 -m 0 -M 99999 -E -1 username
```

Example

```
# chage -I -1 -m 0 -M 99999 -E -1 adam1


# chage -l adam1
Last password change                              : Feb 25, 2018
Password expires                                  : never
Password inactive                                 : never
Account expires                                   : never
Minimum number of days between password change          : 0
Maximum number of days between password change          :
99999
Number of days of warning before password expires       : 7
```

Force user to change password at next login

Syntax

```
# chage -d0 username
```

Example

```
# chage -d0 adam1
```

Lock user

Syntax

```
# usermod -L username
```

Example

```
# usermod -L adam1
```

Unlock user

Syntax

```
# usermod -U username
```

Example

```
# usermod -U adam1
```

UID

Unique User ID better known as UID. For every user that exist on system has UID. UID is numerical representation of every user.   For root user it is 0. For regular users it starts from 1000.

User	UID
root	0
System user	1 – 999
Regular users	1000 +

Groups

Every user we create belongs at least one group and all groups have group ID. **/etc/group** file contains list of all available groups and their member users.

There are two type of groups:-

- Primary group
- Secondary group

Primary group

When you create new user a new group of same name also gets created and the new user become member of that group. This is the group applied to your login and used by default when you create new files and directories. Primary group ID is written in **/etc/passwd** file for respective users in the third field.

Secondary Group
These are the groups users are member other than primary group.

Changing secondary group

```
# usermod -G data2 user1
Where user1 is user and data2 is group and G option for
assigning secondary group
```

Add new group
Syntax

```
# groupadd groupname
```

Example

```
# groupadd data1
```

Delete group
Syntax

```
# groupdel groupname
```

Example

```
# groupdel groupname
```

/etc/group file
/etc/group files stores the group information. There is one entry per line for each group and each line has the fields separated by a colon (:) .

```
groupname:password:GID:grouplist
```

Field	Description
Groupname	Name of group.
password	This is useful to implement privileged groups. Generally, password is not used. It can store encrypted password.
GID	Group ID
Group List	List of all users who are members of the group. Commas must separate the user names.

Example

```
science:x:1003:class1, class2
```

/etc/passwd

passwd file in the /etc directory stores information of all users. The information in /etc/passwd file is required during login. It is a plain text file, which contains list of the system's accounts. Like /etc/group file there is one entry per line for each user, and each line has the fields separated by a colon (:) containing information like user ID, group ID, home directory, shell, etc. Only root user has write permission for this file.

Format

```
username:x:UID:GID:Full_user_name:home_directory:shell
```

Field	Description
Username	Username of the user. It should be unique and can be up to 8 characters. It is also case-sensitive
x	An x character indicates that encrypted password is stored in **/etc/shadow** file.
UID	User ID
GID	Group ID
Full_user_name	Full name of the user
Home directory	Home directory of the user is specified here where user will keep his files.
shell	Default shell for user, normally set to "/bin/bash" but it can be /etc/ksh , /etc/csh or any other shell

Example

```
adam1:x:1004:1004:Adam mark:/home/adam1:/bin/bash
```

/etc/shadow

Stores actual password in encrypted format

Format

```
username:password:last_password_change:minimum
```

Field	Description
Username	Up to 8 characters. Case-sensitive, usually all lowercase. A direct match to the username in the /etc/passwd file.
Password	13 character encrypted password. A blank entry indicates a password is not required to log in (usually a bad idea), and a " * " indicates account has been disabled.
Last_password_change	Date of last password change. Expressed in numbers of days since January 1, 1970
Minimum	The number of days before password may be changed (0 indicates it may be changed at any time)
Maximum	The number of days after which password must be changed (99999 indicates user can keep his or her password unchanged for many, many years)
Warn	Number of days to warn user of an expiring password (7 for a full week)

Inactive	The number of days after password expires that account is disabled
Expire	Date of expiration expressed in number of days since January 1, 1970. (After that Account will disabled)

Example

```
user1:$6$0UseZ0gR$yxl3B9SilhVjpu6epAlir1:17261:0:99999:7:::
```

## Chapter 8

Software management

Every Linux distribution has set of packages that gets installed with installation. As an organization, you may require some more software according to your requirement like you may be using this server as web server so you require Apache. For additional software installation, you require packages. Package is a bundle of all executables and data files in to single file. There are two types of packages are available

1. **Source code packages**
   Bundle of files related to one program, which includes source code, configuration files and documentation.
2. **Binary Packages**
   Binary package is bundle of precompiled binary files and its metadata files.

Package distribution formats

As mentioned packages are of two types, hence distributed in either binary or source code format. The main package distribution systems are :-

Redhat Package Manager
As name suggests this format was introduced by Redhat. This format is not only used by Redhat based distribution like CentOS and Fedora but also adopted by many other distributions like SUSE and Mandriva. RPM packages uses files with .rpm extension.

DEBian package manager

This package distribution system was introduced by Debian. Mainly used by Debian and Debian based distributions like Ubuntu, Linux Mint and PureOS. It uses files with .deb extension.

Source Code Packages

Source code packages can be distributed in to two formats

1. **Tarball files**

   Tarball package distribution is conventional type of package distribution. These type packages are available from any third-party software providers and require **make** utility to compile.

2. **SRPM**

   Redhat based distributions provide repositories from where you can download source code of available binaries we call these files as SRPMS or source RPMs. SRPMs are rpm packages containing only the source code, rpm spec files which can be installed with rpm and then can be compiled or modified manually.

Package metadata

CentOS uses .rpm packages for installing software with rpm command. RPM package is simply a file that contains some files and information about those files. Technically speaking RPM is a file containing **cpio** archive and metadata about itself. RPM Header contains the metadata and this metadata is used to determine following things about the package:-

- Description of package.

- List of files in the package.

- Version and release of package.

- When and who made it.

- Architecture supported.

- Checksums of the files contained in the package.

- Dependences.

  Etc…

Package Management System

If you try to install single package manually you have to first install all its dependences and keep track of versions also. To make software management easy Linux companies had developed a system known as package management system or package manager. Package management system install precompiled packages, which are archives that contains binaries of software, configuration files, and information about dependencies. Package management system is a collection of software tools to automate the process of installation, upgradation and removal of software packages. Software manager maintains its own database of software dependencies and version information. Package management system helps in preventing software mismatches and missing prerequisites. CentOS uses YUM tool for package management.

yum

Like other Linux distributions, CentOS has very comprehensive package management system known as **YUM. Y**ellow dog **U**pdater **M**odifier is command line tool for package management. Yum uses repositories to fetch the correct version of a particular package compatible for your system. Yum allows automatic updating of packages and dependency management. When you use yum command for installation of software, it automatically downloads package and all its dependencies from defined repositories.

Repository

Yum repository is collection of RPM packages with metadata that is used by Yum Command. It can be present locally (DVD, directory) or remotely (FTP, HTTP, HTTPS). The package manager uses repositories to install, remove, and upgrade packages. The configuration file for yum repositories is **/etc/yum.conf**. To define repositories you can use this file. However, it is recommended to create or use existing **.repo** file in the **/etc/yum.repos.d/** directory for defining repositories. There are two type of repositories, CentOS official repositories and third party repositories. When you install CentOS it comes with three official repositories predefined and enabled

- Centos Base
- Centos Extra
- Centos updates

Other than these three repositories, CentOS community provide more repositories which can be enabled. The list is given bellow

- CentOSPlus
- CentOS-Fasttrack
- Software Collections
- Continuous Release (CR)
- debuginfo

List of some of the main third party repositories is given bellow:

- EPEL Repository Mirrors
- nux-dextop
- ElRepo
- LinuxTECH.NET
- IUS Community

Command to explore repositories

Display all enabled repositories

```
# yum repolist
```

Display all repositories enabled and disabled

```
# yum repolist all
```

Add / Enable / Disable repositories

Using yum-config-manager command

Add repository

Repositories usually provide their own .repo file for repository configutaion. To add repository which provides. repo file you can use this command

```
# yum-config-manager --add-repo repository_url
```

Enable defined repository

You can use yum-config-manager command to enable defined repository. In this example we will enable CentOS fasttrack defined repository .

List enabled repositories

```
# yum repolist enabled
```

```
[root@centos1 ~]# yum repolist enabled
Loaded plugins: fastestmirror, langpacks
Loading mirror speeds from cached hostfile
 * base: del-mirrors.extreme-ix.org
 * extras: del-mirrors.extreme-ix.org
 * updates: del-mirrors.extreme-ix.org
repo id                                    repo name
base/7/x86_64                              CentOS-7 - Base
extras/7/x86_64                            CentOS-7 - Extras
updates/7/x86_64                           CentOS-7 - Updates
repolist: 11,908
```

List all repositories including defined

```
# yum repolist all
```

List all repositories and grep only fasttrack

```
#yum repolist all |grep fast
```

```
[root@centos1 ~]# yum repolist all |grep fast
Loaded plugins: fastestmirror, langpacks
C7.0.1406-fasttrack/x86_64        CentOS-7.0.1406 - CentOSPlus        disabled
C7.1.1503-fasttrack/x86_64        CentOS-7.1.1503 - CentOSPlus        disabled
C7.2.1511-fasttrack/x86_64        CentOS-7.2.1511 - CentOSPlus        disabled
!fasttrack/7/x86_64               CentOS-7 - fasttrack                disabled
```

Now we know the exact name of repository we will enable it

```
# yum-config-manager --enable "CentOS-7 - fasttrack"
```

Now check enabled repositories

```
# yum repolist enabled
```

```
[root@centos1 ~]# yum repolist enabled
Loaded plugins: fastestmirror, langpacks
Loading mirror speeds from cached hostfile
 * base: del-mirrors.extreme-ix.org
 * extras: del-mirrors.extreme-ix.org
 * fasttrack: del-mirrors.extreme-ix.org
 * updates: del-mirrors.extreme-ix.org
repo id                                    repo name
!base/7/x86_64                             CentOS-7 - Base
!extras/7/x86_64                           CentOS-7 - Extras
!fasttrack/7/x86_64                        CentOS-7 - fasttrack
!updates/7/x86_64                          CentOS-7 - Updates
repolist: 11,908
```

Disable repository

To disable a particular repository

Syntax

```
# yum-config-manager --disable "name of repository"
```

Example

```
# yum-config-manager --disable "CentOS-7 - fasttrack"
```

Enable third party repository

As mentioned we can add third party repositories which are maintained by CentOS community. In this example we will install EPEL repository. EPEL repository is managed by the EPEL group. The EPEL is an abbreviation that stands for **E**xtra **P**ackages for **E**nterprise **L**inux. Installing and enabling EPEL repository is very simple in CentOS. Use yum command to install package epel-release

```
# yum install -y epel-release
```

Now check it

```
# yum repolist enabled
```

repo file

Configuration files for yum repositories are located in /etc/yum.repos.d/ directory having .repo extension. This repository configuration file has following options :-

Repository ID	One word unique repository ID
Name	Human readable string describing the repository

Baseurl	URL to the repodata directory of repository is located.
Gpgcheck	Enable/disable GPG signature checking
Gpgkey	URL to the GPG key file for a repository
Exclude	List of the packages to exclude
Includepkgs	List of packages that yum can see
Enabled	Enable/Disable repository

Required fields are:

- Repository ID
- Name
- Baseurl
- Enabled

Example

```
[cr]
name=CentOS-$releasever - cr
baseurl=http://mirror.centos.org/centos/$releasever/cr/$basearch/
gpgcheck=1
gpgkey=file:///etc/pki/rpm-gpg/RPM-GPG-KEY-CentOS-7
enabled=0
```

CentOS DVD ISO as YUM Repository

CentOS DVD provides many software. When you are working with VPS physical DVD is not available, you can use CentOS DVD as repository. To make CentOS ISO image as repository following steps are there

1. Download the ISO image directly on your server or transfer it. To download image file directly from any mirror of CentOS using **wget** command

```
# wget http://centos.mirror.net.in/centos/7/isos/x86_64/CentOS-7-x86_64-DVD-1708.iso
```

2. Mount CentOS DVD ISO

```
mount -o loop /path_to_iso   /mnt
```

3. Create .repo repository configuration file

/etc/yum.repos.d/centosiso.repo

```
[installmedia]
name=CentOS Linux 7 DVD
baseurl=file:///mnt/
gpgcheck=1
gpgkeys=file:///mnt/RPM-GPG-KEY-CentOS-7
enabled=1
```

Custom Repository

To make your own custom repository from downloaded RPM packages, the steps are following :-

1. Create directory for your custom repository.

```
mkdir /myrepo
```

2. Transfer/ download files to this directory

```
# wget http://mirror.centos.org/centos/7/os/x86_64/Packages/GeoIP-1.5.0-
11.el7.i686.rpm
```

3. Use **createrepo** to create repodata

```
# createrepo /myrepo
```

4. Create configuration files

/etc/yum.repos.d/mycustom.repo

Below is example of custom repo file

```
[mycustomrepo]
name=Custom Repository
baseurl=file:///myrepo/
enabled=1
gpgcheck=0
```

Package management using Yum

Install package

Syntax

```
# yum install -y package_name
```

Example

```
# yum install -y firefox
```

Remove package

Syntax

```
# yum remove package_name
```

Example

```
# yum remove firefox
```

Check which package provides specific file

```
# yum provides file-name
```

Example

```
# yum provides /etc/hosts
```

Get help

```
# yum help
```

List all installed and available software

```
# yum list
```

List all installed software

```
# yum list installed
```

Search the package name with keyword

Syntax

```
# yum search keyword
```

Example

```
# yum search bzip2
```

Display information about the package

Syntax

```
# yum info package_name
```

Example

```
# yum info zip
```

Check for Available Updates

```
# yum check-update
```

Update all software provided by enabled repositories

```
# yum update
```

Clean the yum cache

```
# yum clean all
```

Interactive shell

```
# yum shell
```

List yum history

```
# yum history list
```

Package group

Package group is group of software, which have same motive to install such as development tools, web server, desktop etc. It makes administrator's life easy by installing and downloading dependent software automatically. For example, you want to install backup client you will give command **yum group install "Backup Client"**

List all package group available

```
# yum group list
```

Install group package

Syntax

```
yum group install package_name
```

Example

```
# yum group install "Backup Client"
```

Remove package group

Syntax

```
yum group remove package_name
```

Example

```
# yum group remove "Backup Client"
```

Information about group package

Syntax

```
# yum group info package_name
```

Example

```
# yum group info "Development Tools"
```

Package management using RPM

RPM stands for **R**ed Hat **P**ackage **M**anager. RPM packages have **.rpm** extension. **rpm** command is used to manage software which include listing, installing, updating and removing rpm packages. RPM is usually used to install packages that have been downloaded locally

Install

Syntax

```
rpm -ihv  package_name
```

Example

```
# rpm -ihv zip-3.0-11.el7.x86_64.rpm
```

Update

Syntax

```
rpm -Uhv package_name
```

Example

```
# rpm -Uhv zip-3.0-11.el7.x86_64.rpm
```

Remove

Syntax

```
rpm -ev package_name
```

Example

```
# rpm -ev zip
```

Query all installed packages

Syntax

```
rpm -qa
```

Display detailed information about package

Syntax

```
rpm -qi package_name
```

Example

```
rpm -qi zip
```

Find the file belongs to which package

Syntax

```
rpm -qf  path_to_the_file
```

Example

```
# rpm -qf /etc/hosts
setup-2.8.71-4.el7.noarch
```

Find out all dependences

Syntax

```
rpm -qpR package_name
```

Example

```
# rpm -qpR zip-3.0-11.el7.x86_64.rpm
libbz2.so.1()(64bit)
libc.so.6()(64bit)
libc.so.6(GLIBC_2.14)(64bit)
libc.so.6(GLIBC_2.2.5)(64bit)
libc.so.6(GLIBC_2.3)(64bit)
libc.so.6(GLIBC_2.3.4)(64bit)
libc.so.6(GLIBC_2.4)(64bit)
<- Output Truncated ->
```

## Chapter 9

Managing services

When you boot your system, it starts and stops some services to achieve required state of the system. Suppose you want to start the system in GUI mode, system has to start all the services related to Desktop environment, same way if you have configured the server as web server you have to start the web services during boot process. Even to do its basic tasks it requires many services to be running like network, date and time etc. **SysV** was service manager used in the previous versions of CentOS. **SysV** use to start services one by one at boot time that means next service will start once previous service finished starting. In CentOS version 7 Systemd has been introduced.

Introduction to systemd

Systemd is a system and service manager for CentOS 7. It is backward compatible with SysV init scripts. It provides number of new features like:-

- Parallel startup of system service at boot time
- On demand activation of devices
- Dependency based service control logic
- Path-based activation: on demand activation of services when a particular file or directory changes its state
- Device based activation (like USB)
- Earlier BOOT Logging

Before systemd, previous versions of CentOS used SysV scripts located in the **/etc/rc.d/init.d/** directory to control the system state. In CentOS 7, these init scripts have been replaced with service units, service units reside in **/etc/systemd/system/** directory. Service units end with the **.service** file extension. **systemctl** command is used to view, start, stop, restart, enable, or disable system services. If you are coming from previous version of CentOS/ Redhat, earlier there use to be more than one command for service management, like for service status management **service** command and for service startup management **chkconfig** command. However, in version 7 it has been replaced by single command **systemtl**.

Service Status Management

Detail	Command
Starts a service	`systemctl start `*`name.service`* Example `systemctl start iscsi.service`
Stops a service	`systemctl stop `*`name.service`* Example `systemctl stop iscsi.service`

Restarts a service	`systemctl restart name.service`
	Example
	`systemctl restart iscsi.service`

Restarts a service only if it is running.	`systemctl try-restart`
	`name.service`
	Example
	`systemctl try-restart iscsi.service`

Reloads configuration	`systemctl reload `*`name.service`*

	Example
	`systemctl reload iscsi.service`
Checks if a service is running.	`systemctl status name.service`
	`systemctl is-active name.service`
	Example
	`systemctl status iscsi.service`
	`systemctl is-active iscsi.service`
Displays the status of all service	`systemctl list-units --type service --all`
	or
	`systemctl -at service`

Like **chkconfig** in earlier versions, you can use the **systemctl** to control the services during system boot.

Enable and disable service at startup

Task	Command
Enable service	`systemctl enable name.service`
	Example
	`systemctl enable iscsi.service`
Disable service	`systemctl disable name.service`
	Example
	`systemctl disable iscsi.service`
To prevent service from starting dynamically or even manually unless unmasked	`systemctl mask name.service`
	Example
	`systemctl mask iscsi.service`
Check whether a service enabled or not	`systemctl is-enabled name.service`

	Example
	`systemctl is-enabled iscsi.service`
Lists all services and check if they are enabled or not	`systemctl list-unit-files --type service`

Service unit information

When we give command `systemctl -status name.service.`

It provides following information

Field	Description
Loaded	Whether the service unit is loaded, the absolute path to the unit file, whether the unit is enabled.
Active	Running or not
Main PID	PID of the service
Process	Information about process
CGroup	information about Control Groups.

Example

```
# systemctl status abrt-ccpp.service
abrt-ccpp.service - Install ABRT coredump hook
    Loaded: loaded (/usr/lib/systemd/system/abrt-ccpp.service;
enabled)
    Active: active (exited) since Sat 2017-03-18 06:05:25 IST;
1h 7min ago
  Process: 1013 ExecStart=/usr/sbin/abrt-install-ccpp-hook
install (code=exited, status=0/SUCCESS)
 Main PID: 1013 (code=exited, status=0/SUCCESS)
    CGroup: /system.slice/abrt-ccpp.service
```

Managing services

To list all services and there status

```
# systemctl -at service
```

To list current setting of specific service

Syntax

```
systemctl status name.service
```

Example

```
# systemctl status httpd.service
```

Enabling service

Syntax

```
systemctl enable name.service
```

Example

```
# systemctl enable iscsi.service
```

To disable service

Syntax

```
systemctl disable name.service
```

Example

```
# systemctl disable iscsi.service
```

Determine status of service

Syntax

```
# systemctl status name.service
```

Example

```
# systemctl status httpdd.service
```

Starting service

Syntax

```
# systemctl start name.service
```

Example

```
# systemctl start httpd.service
```

Stopping service

Syntax

```
# systemctl stop name.service
```

Example

```
# systemctl stop httpd.service
```

Restarting service

Syntax

```
# systemctl restart name.service
```

Example

```
# systemctl restart httpd.service
```

Install new service

Procedure to install new service

1. Install new service package

```
# yum install service_name
```

2. Configure the service to start automatically at startup

```
# systemctl enable name.service
```

3. Start the service

```
# systemctl start name.service
```

Example

```
# yum install httpd
# systemctl enable httpd.service
# systemctl start httpd.service
```

systemd Targets

Previous versions of CentOS implemented run levels. Run level is state or mode of OS in which it will run. Each run level causes certain number of services to be stopped or started, providing control over behavior of machine. However, in CentOS 7 it is replaced by **systemd targets.** There were seven **Runlevels** in previous version of CentOS, which has been replaced by corresponding **target units** in new version

Run level	Description	Target unit
0	Halt the machine	poweroff.target
1	Single user mode	rescue.target
2	Multiuser with command line no GUI	multiuser.target

3	Multiuser with command line no GUI	multiuser.target
4	Multiuser with command line no GUI	multiuser.target
5	Multiuser with GUI	graphical.target
6	Reboot	reboot.target

List currently loaded target

```
# systemctl list-units --type target
```

```
[root@centos1 ~]# ls -la /etc/systemd/system/default.target
lrwxrwxrwx. 1 root root 36 Feb 16 23:57 /etc/systemd/system/default.target -> /lib/systemd/system/graphical.target
```

Default Target

Default target decides the direction in which **systemd** process takes the system at boot time. The file **/etc/inittab** is no longer used to set the default run level as it was in earlier version of CentOS. Now default target unit is represented by the **/etc/systemd/system/default.target** file. This file is a symbolic link to current set target. Suppose current target is set to graphical, this file will be symbolic link to graphical target file

Change default target
Syntax
```
# systemctl set-default <name of target>.target
```
Example
```
# systemctl set-default graphical.target
Removed symlink /etc/systemd/system/default.target.
Created symlink from /etc/systemd/system/default.target to
/usr/lib/systemd/system/graphical.target.
```

Viewing the Default Target

```
# systemctl get-default
```

Changing the Current Target

After changing default target, the current target remains unchanged until next reboot. To change the current target without reboot use

Syntax

```
# systemctl isolate default
Or
# systemctl default
```

To Change the current target to different target other than default target. Suppose you want to start the single user target

Syntax

```
# systemctl isolate newtarget.target
```

Example

```
# systemctl isoloate rescue.target
```

## Chapter 10

OpenSSH

SSH(Secure Shell) provides a secure channel over unsecure network in client server architecture. SSH is a replacement of telnet, which is insecure protocol. It allows secure channel to login and execute command remotely because all communication between client and server is encrypted. CentOS includes the OpenSSH package for ssh. The OpenSSH suite comes with CentOS is SSH version 2. OpenSSH provides number of tools for secure communication like ssh, scp and sftp. It also offers capabilities for secure tunneling, different authentication methods, and easy configuration. CentOS version 7 includes **openssh**, **openssh-server** and **openssh-clients** packages. The openssh package also requires openssl-libs to be installed on the system, as it provides cryptographic libraries for encrypted communication. The default installation of CentOS comes with openssh preinstalled. If is not there, you need to install them with this command.

```
# yum install openssh openssh-server openssh-clients openssl-libs
```

Start the service
```
# systemctl start sshd.service
```

Enable the service to start automatically on system boot
```
# systemctl enable sshd.service
```

Check the status

```
# systemctl status sshd.service
```

Versions of SSH protocol

There are two varieties of SSH ,version 1 and version 2. The OpenSSH suite comes under CentOS 7 is SSH version 2. SSH2 is a more secure, also includes SFTP, which is functionally similar to FTP, but with encryption.

Configuration file

File	Description
/etc/ssh/sshd_config	The default configuration file for the sshd daemon
/etc/ssh/ssh_config	The default configuration file for SSH client. it will be overridden, if **~/.ssh/config** exists
~/.ssh/config	The client-side configuration file

Connecting from client

If you are on the Linux client machine and you want to login on to remote CentOS server you require ssh client installed on your client machine and SSH server running on CentOS server. From client give this command

```
$ ssh -x user@serverIPaddress_or_hostname
```

Example

```
$ ssh -x root@centos1
The authenticity of host 'centos1 (192.168.131.152)' can't be
established.
```

```
ECDSA key fingerprint is
SHA256:kJkcVAsgMdv5FsbEeaHWNK33LJHHLaHSUC8WZE/Sri8.
Are you sure you want to continue connecting (yes/no)? yes
Warning: Permanently added 'centos1,192.168.131.152' (ECDSA)
to the list of known hosts.
root@centos1's password:
[root@centos1 ~]
```

It will ask password of the user name specified in the ssh command. When ssh connection from client to server is made first time, the public key of server is stored locally on the client, so it's identity can be verified next time.

Ctrl + d or **exit** command will terminate **ssh** session.

To connect MS windows client to CentOS server you require third party software like **putty**.

ssh keys
ssh keys helps in identifying yourself to an server using public key cryptography and challenge response authentication. ssh keys are generated in pairs known, one as public and other as private key. The public is for sharing and private key is for you. It must be kept safely. Server having public key can send challenge, which can only be answered by client holding private key. This allows password less login.

Passwordless Login Using SSH Keys
SSH also allows you to connect from trusted SSH client to SSH server without password. In this section, we will learn how to do passwordless

login from Linux client to Linux server. In bellow example, **centos1** is Linux client and **centos2** act as Linux server.

1. Create keys on **centos1** host

```
[root@centos1 ~]# ssh-keygen
```

2. Copy public key from **centos1** to second server **centos2** host

```
# scp ~/.ssh/id_rsa.pub root@centos2:/root/id_rsa.server1.pub
```

3. On second server **centos2** create directory .ssh in the home directory in our case the user is root its home directory is /root and change the permissions to **700** (only owner can read, write and execute) .

```
[root@centos2 ~]# mkdir .ssh
[root@centos2 ~]# chmod 700 .ssh
```

4. Append the public key earlier copied in /root directory file to **authorized_keys** file and change permissions.

```
[root@centos2 ~]# cat id_rsa.server1.pub >> .ssh/authorized_keys
[root@centos2 ~]# chmod 644 .ssh/authorized_keys
```

5. Now try login from **centos1** to server **centos2** it will not ask for password.

```
[root@centos1 ~]# ssh root@centos2
```

scp Utility

scp is part of openssh suit which can be used to transfer files between machines over a encrypted connection. It is secure alternative to rcp command. Syntax for scp command is :-

Syntax

```
scp filename username@hostname:/directory
```

Example

If you want to transfer abc.txt from host1 ie. **centos1** to remote machine **centos2**. On centos1 shell prompt type:-

```
centos1~]$ scp abc.txt user1@centos2:.
```

To transfer a file from remote machine to the local system

Syntax:

```
scp username@hostname:remotefile localdirectory
```

Example

In this example we will transfer xyz.txt from remote host2 ie. centos2 to local machine centos1. On centos1 shell prompt

```
centos1~]$ scp user2@centos2:/home/user2/xyz.txt /home/user1/.
```

sftp Utility

File Transfer Protocol (FTP) is widely used protocol for transferring files between computers specially for downloading files from internet. However, it uses unencrypted communication, which is not secure. SSH File Transfer Protocol (SFTP) is a SSH implementation for FTP that provides encrypted data transfer. sftp provides interactive prompt. You can use command to download or upload file to remote host.

To connect to a remote system using **sftp username@hostname or IP address** of server it will ask the password for username

Syntax

```
sftp username@hostname
```

Example

```
# sftp user1@centos2
```

```
[user1@centos1 ~]$
[user1@centos1 ~]$ sftp user1@centos2
The authenticity of host 'centos2 (192.168.131.152)' can't be established.
ECDSA key fingerprint is 30:ab:8c:ec:38:aa:36:80:b9:4d:c5:dc:01:ff:00:bf.
Are you sure you want to continue connecting (yes/no)? yes
Warning: Permanently added 'centos2,192.168.131.152' (ECDSA) to the list of known hosts.
user1@centos2's password:
Connected to centos2.
sftp>
```

Common Commands for sftp

Command	Description
?	help
ls	List the content of remote directory
lls	List the content of local directory
cd	Change the remote directory
lcd	Change local directory
mkdir *directoryname*	Make directory at remote server
lmdir *directoryname*	Make local directory
rmdir *directoryname*	Remove remote directory
put *filename*	Transfer file to remote server
mput files	Transfer multiple files to remote machine
get *filename*	Download file to local machine
mget files	Download multiple files
bye	Quite sftp
! command	Run shell command

Examples

Getting help

```
sftp> ?
Available commands:
bye                     Quit sftp
cd path                 Change remote directory to 'path'
chgrp grp path          Change group of file 'path' to 'grp'
[...output truncated.. ]
```

Uploading single file

Transferring file from local to remote machine

```
sftp> put xyz.txt
Uploading xyz.txt to /home/user1/xyz.txt
xyz.txt                           100% 1508     1.5KB/s   00:00
```

Uploading multiple files

```
sftp> mput *.txt
Uploading 11.txt to /home/user1/11.txt
11.txt                     100% 1663     1.6KB/s   00:00
Uploading a2.txt to /home/user1/a2.txt
a2.txt                  100% 1715    1.7KB/s   00:00
```

Downloading single file

Transfer file from remote to local machine

```
sftp> get abc.txt
Fetching /home/user1/abc.txt to abc.txt
/home/user1/abc.txt              100% 1508     1.5KB/s   00:00
```

Downloading multiple files

```
sftp> mget *.txt
```

Changing Directories

To change from one directory to another directory

On remote machine.

```
sftp> cd Documents
```

On Local machine

```
sftp> lcd Downloads
```

Create new Directory

On remote Machine

```
sftp> mkdir julli
```

On local Machine

```
sftp> lmkdir David
```

Remove Directories

```
sftp> rmdir julli
```

Exit sFTP

```
sftp> bye
```

## Chapter 11

VNC

VNC Virtual Network Computing is graphical desktop sharing system. It is used to get GUI desktop of Linux server remotely. In VNC there two parts, one is VNC server other is VNC client. VNC server runs on CentOS server and client runs on MS Windows or Linux workstation. X Server runs on CentOS server where as VNC client shows only copy of the display.

To configure VNC on server who's desktop you want to share

1. install

```
# yum install tigervnc-server
```

2. Copy file from **/lib/systemd/system/vncserver@.service** to **/etc/systemd/system/vncserver@:2.service**

```
cp /lib/systemd/system/vncserver@.service /etc/systemd/system/vncserver@:2.service
```

3. Edit **/etc/systemd/system/vncserver@:2.service** change <USER> with the local user which will connect to VNC server

```
ExecStartPre=/bin/sh -c '/usr/bin/vncserver -kill %i > /dev/null 2>&1 || :'
ExecStart=/sbin/runuser -l <USER> -c "/usr/bin/vncserver %i"
PIDFile=/home/<USER>/.vnc/%H%i.pid
ExecStop=/bin/sh -c '/usr/bin/vncserver -kill %i > /dev/null 2>&1 || :'
"/lib/systemd/system/vncserver@.service" 45L, 1744C
```

Change to following in my case it is user1

87

```
ExecStartPre=/bin/sh -c '/usr/bin/vncserver -kill %i > /dev/null 2>&1 || :'
ExecStart=/sbin/runuser -l user1 -c "/usr/bin/vncserver %i"
PIDFile=/home/user1/.vnc/%H%i.pid
ExecStop=/bin/sh -c '/usr/bin/vncserver -kill %i > /dev/null 2>&1 || :'
```

4. Set VNC password

```
# su user_name
# vncpasswd
```

5. Start and enable the VNC service

```
# systemctl start vncserver@:2.service
# systemctl enable vncserver@:2.service
```

6. Open firewall for vncserver

```
firewall-cmd --permanent --add-service vnc-server
firewall-cmd --reload
```

7. Install vncviewer on the remote machine

```
# yum install tigervnc
```

8. Connect on remote machine

Go to Desktop of linux box open terminal

```
# vncviewer servername:2
```

It will ask for password we had set for vncuser, give password.

## Chapter 12

Web server

A webserver is program, which allows web browser clients to access web pages. It uses HTTP (Hypertext Transfer Protocol). In CentOS Apache HTTP server can be used as Web Server.

Deploying http server

Installation of Apache web server includes following steps

1. Installation
2. Start service
3. Enable the service to start at boot time
4. Firewall configuration
5. Test

Install http server

```
# yum install httpd
```

Start service

```
# systemctl start httpd
```

Enable the service to start on boot

```
# systemctl enable httpd
```

Open firewall port and reload its configuration

```
# firewall-cmd --permanent --add-service=http
# firewall-cmd --reload
```

Default directory where http keeps contents

```
/var/www/html
```

Configuration file

```
/etc/httpd/conf/httpd.conf
```

Directory for additional configuration files that are included in the main configuration file.

```
/etc/httpd/conf.d/
```

Verifying Configuration

After changing configuration, verify it before using:-

```
# apachectl configtest
```

If you change the configuration files, you have to restart/reload the service, for that refer the **Restarting service** section.

Test

1. Create file in directory /var/www/html/index.html and Write **Hello**

2. Save the file and exit

3. Open the Firefox and on the address bar write http://localhost

4. You should see hello

Stopping the Service

To stop running httpd service

```
# systemctl stop httpd
```

To prevent http service from starting automatically at boot time

```
# systemctl disable httpd
```

Restarting service

There are three ways to restart the service httpd

1. Complete restart using systemctl command

```
# systemctl restart httpd
```

2. Reload only configuration, in case you have changed the configuration. In this case, all request during reload will be denied including active requests also.

```
# systemctl reload httpd
```

3. To reload configuration without affecting active requests

```
# apachectl gracefull
```

Verifying the service

To verify the service if it is active

```
# systemctl is-active httpd
```

Virtual Hosts

The Apache HTTP Server offers option to create multiple websites on single webserver using virtual hosts. Based on host name, IP address or port number, virtual hosts allows same webserver to provide different information. You can host multiple websites on a single machine with a single IP using virtual hosting. Virtual hosting is suitable for shared web hosting environments, where multiple websites are hosted on a single server.

Steps to host multiple sites on single server using virtual hosting:-

1. Create the directory structure
2. Create test web pages for each host
3. Set ownership and permissions
4. Change SELinux context of files
5. Configure your virtual host directories
6. Change the Apache configuration file
7. Create virtual host configuration files
8. Verify the configuration files and restart the httpd service
9. Create DNS record in /etc/hosts file or in the DNS server
10. Test the virtual hosts

Steps in detail

In this example, we will host two websites abc_example.com and xyz_example.com.

1. Create Directory Structure

First, create directory for each website to hold html files. This directory is known as document root for each website

```
# mkdir -p /var/www/html/abc_example.com
# mkdir -p /var/www/html/xyz_example.com
```

2. Create test web pages for each host

```
# vi /var/www/html/abc_example.com/index.html
```

Add following content

```
Abc_example.com
```

Save the file and exit from vi

Same way

```
# vi /var/www/html/xyz_example.com/index.html
```

Add following content

```
Xyz_example.com
```

Save the file and exit from vi

3. Set ownership and permissions

Set the ownership of newly created directories to apache user and group

```
# chown -R apache:apache /var/www/html/abc_example.com
# chown -R apache:apache /var/www/html/xyz_example.com
```

Change the /var/www/html folder readable by world

```
# chmod -R 755 /var/www/html
```

4. Change SELinux context of files

If SELinux is enabled in the system change context of newly created directories.

```
 # semanage fcontext -a -t httpd_sys_content_t
"/var/www/html/abc_example.com(/.*)?"
# semanage fcontext -a -t httpd_sys_content_t
"/var/www/html/xyz_example.com(/.*)?"
# restorecon -R -v /var/www/html/
```

Verify the context

```
# ls -laZ /var/www/html/
```

5. Configure your virtual host configuration directories

Create two directories for configuration files for virtual sites one directory is for all configured websites (sites-available) and another to hold symbolic links to virtual hosts that will be published (sites-enabled).

```
# mkdir -p /etc/httpd/sites-available
# mkdir -p /etc/httpd/sites-enabled
```

6. Change Apache configuration file

Edit the main configuration file (/etc/httpd/conf/httpd.conf) to include new configuration directory (sites-enabled) so that Apache will look for virtual hosts in this directory.

```
# vi /etc/httpd/conf/httpd.conf
```

Add this line at the very end of the file:

```
IncludeOptional sites-enabled/*.conf
```

Save the file and exit from vi

7. Create virtual host configuration files

Create configuration files for each virtual host

```
# vi /etc/httpd/sites-available/abc_example.com.conf
```
```
<VirtualHost *:80>
    ServerName www.abc_example.com
    ServerAlias abc_example.com
    DocumentRoot /var/www/html/abc_example.com
</VirtualHost>
```

```
# vi /etc/httpd/sites-available/xyz_example.com.conf
```

```
<VirtualHost *:80>
    ServerName www.xyz_example.com
    ServerAlias xyz_example.com
    DocumentRoot /var/www/html/xyz_example.com
</VirtualHost>
```

Create soft links of virtual host configuration files in **sites-enabled** directory (Note this command is in single line, due to page width limitation it wrapped to next line. When you issue this command issue it in single line)

```
# ln -s /etc/httpd/sites-available/abc_example.com.conf
/etc/httpd/sites-enabled/abc_example.com.conf
```

```
# ln -s /etc/httpd/sites-available/xyz_example.com.conf
/etc/httpd/sites-enabled/xyz_example.com.conf
```

8. Verify the configuration files and restart the httpd service

Verify the configuration files

```
# apachectl configtest
```

Restart Service

```
# systemctl restart httpd
```

6. Create DNS record in /etc/hosts file or in the DNS server

If you have DNS server you can add the entries for

```
www.abc_example.com
www.xyz_example.com
```

For testing purpose you can add the entries in /etc/hosts

```
vi /etc/hosts
```

```
192.168.131.152    www.abc_example.com
192.168.131.152    www.zyz_example.com
```

7. Test the new websites (virtual hosts)

Open your web browser on CentOS Server in GUI Mode and go to the URLs

http://www.abc_example.com

and

http://www.xyz_example.com.

You will see the content of each website

## Chapter 13

Exploring Shell

Shell

A shell is a command-line interpreter. It is interface between user and Operating system. User gives command on Shell prompt and operating system executes that command. As shell is a command language interpreter, the basic purpose of shell is to translate human readable commands typed at a terminal into system actions. A shell is a special user program through which other programs are invoked. The shell gets started when the user logs in or start the terminal. Although there are several different shells like Bash, Korn, C shell etc, Bash is the default shell for Linux. Based on the shell you use there are minor differences in commands also.

Shell Script

Generally, we use shell in interactive mode, where user inputs command and gets output. However, some time you use shell scripts. Shell script is script you write to give series of command. Scripts that are more complex check conditions and run loops. Seasoned administrators use shell scripts to automate administrative tasks and to monitor system. Suppose, you want to check the disk space, memory availability and environment variables before invoking a program. There are two ways to do it, either you can give all commands manually every time before running that program or you can use shell script to do that. Shell scripts generally end with **sh** extension. Figure bellow shows an example of shell script

```
user1@MyLinux ~ $
user1@MyLinux ~ $ cat /usr/share/doc/acpid/examples/ac.sh
#!/bin/sh
# /etc/acpid/ac.sh
# Detect loss of AC power and regaining of AC power, and take action
# appropriately.

# On my laptop anyway, this script doesn't not get different parameters for
# loss of power and regained power. So, I have to use a separate program to
# tell what the adapter status is.

# This uses the spicctrl program for probing the sonypi device.
BACKLIGHT=$(spicctrl -B)

if on_ac_power; then
        # Now on AC power.

        # Tell longrun to go crazy.
        longrun -f performance
        longrun -s 0 100

        # Turn up the backlight unless it's up far enough.
        if [ "$BACKLIGHT" -tt 108 ]; then
                spicctrl -b 108
        fi
else
        # Now off AC power.

        # Tell longrun to be a miser.
        longrun -f economy
        longrun -s 0 50 # adjust to suite..

        # Don't allow the screen to be too bright, but don't turn the
        # backlight up, on removal, and don't turn it all the way down, as
        # that is unusable on my laptop in most conditions. Adjust to
        # taste.
        if [ "$BACKLIGHT" -gt 68 ]; then
                spicctrl -b 68
        fi
fi
user1@MyLinux ~ $
```

Command line Interface

Command line interface (CLI) is way to access the shell. If you do
CentOS installation without GUI or Minimal, you will get only command
line interface through virtual terminals. When you install Linux with GUI
you have two option to access CLI

- Virtual Terminals
- Graphical Terminal

Virtual Terminals

Virtual Terminal is full screen command line interface. If you are
working on CentOS server locally, you will get more than one Virtual
terminal running on same server. Having more than one virtual terminal
allows the administrator to switch to another terminal if necessary.
Even if you have Graphical Desktop environment is installed you can
still access virtual terminals. Virtual terminals can be accessed on

CentOS System by pressing Ctrl+Alt+F2 till F6. To come back to the graphical session, press Ctrl+Alt+F1. On pressing Ctrl+Alt+F2 you will get first Virtual terminal like that

```
CentOS Linux 7 (Core)
Kernel 3.10.0-514.el7.x86_64 on an x86_64

centos1 login: _
```

Login and start issuing commands

Graphical Terminal Emulator

System with Graphical desktop environment can get CLI inside GUI with **Terminal Emulator.** Terminal allows you to open a window and lets you interact with the shell. Depending on Graphical Desktop environment installed on Linux distributions you have bunch of terminal emulator available like gnome-terminal, konsole, rxvt, xterm, LXterminal, guake, terminator, tilde, yakuake etc. Gnome-terminal is the default terminal emulator for CentOS Linux with GNOME desktop environment. To start Gnome terminal, press Activities and press terminal icon.

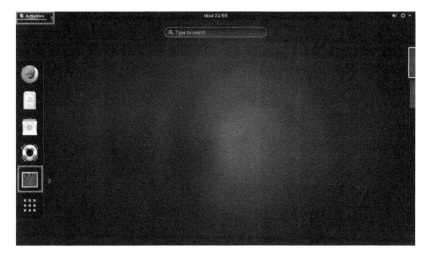

Command prompt

Although you can customize the prompt, but more often you will get either # or $ at end of prompt. Where # indicates the user is logged in as root (administrator) user and $ prompt as normal user. You can display additional information in the prompt like username, current directory and server name even you can show current date and time.

Structure of commands

Normally if you run command from the shell prompt will have the following format:

```
command -options <filename>
```

Example

```
tail -f myfile
```

However, file name is not used in all commands. in some commands only command or command and options are used

```
ls -la
```

Tips for the bash shell

Whether you are on virtual terminal or using Terminal emulator, command format is same. Following are some of the useful features of bash shell you can use in day-to-day tasks

TAB completion

Tab completion is one of the most useful feature of Bash shell. It has ability to guess the command, directory or file name by pressing TAB after writing partial command, directory or file name. Shell will automatically complete the word if only one option is present otherwise it will offers all possible completions. For example, suppose you want to change directory to **abc** you write **cd ab** and press TAB, the system will complete the word automatically.

Bash History

Shell saves the command you have given on shell in a file in your home directory. You can check the last commands by giving **history** command.

```
$ history
```

If you want to give last command again, you can press UP arrow key and then press **ENTER** key. You can press **UP** arrow key repeatedly to scroll backward in the history of commands.

Wildcards

Wildcards or wild characters are symbols represents one or more characters in the shell command. Most common wild card characters are

*   Star

?   Question mark

[]   Square baskets

Where

Star (*)

Represents zero or more characters

Example

```
$ ls b*
```

List all files starting with b

Question mark (?)

Represents single character

Example

```
$ ls ?at
```

List all files whose first letter of file name can be any character like bat, cat or hat

Square brackets

Represent a range of characters

Example

ls b[1-5]

List all files starting with b and second character should be numeric character starting from 1 to 5. It can b1, b2, b3, b4 and b5

Check the current shell

```
# echo $SHELL
```

## Chapter 14

Backup and Restore

Backup of your computer data is always important to prevent data loss. Backup saves you in case of data loss. There are many reasons for data loss like hard disk failure, OS failure, virus, malware or due to human error. Before taking actual backup you should try to answer three W's : what, when and where

What

In my experience as an administrator if you ask any user what part of data is important for backup, the simple, answer will be whole data. As an administrator, you should understand it is ideal to take backup of whole system daily but in practical, you require large device which can accommodate the whole data. Moreover taking backup also takes time. Suppose if you are taking backup of server which is online and you want to take backup of whole system, it may take hours to finish. In this case, by the time you are on verge of finishing the backup half of the data has already changed. Therefore, data insistency arises. Best way to take consistent data backup is to stop the whole system and then take backup but if your backup window is large, then it is very difficult to get down time of production systems. The solution for this problem is to segregate the data in to two or more parts. First part of data that is changing regularly. Second, the data that changes once a while. The best example of that is, in normal production environment you have software binary files that changes very rarely and data files which gets updated regularly. You can take backup of whole system monthly or quarterly and take backup of data files daily.

Where

Next question is where you want to keep backup. There two part of this question first part is device on which you want to take backup. It can be external hard disk, tape drive, DVD or even USB drive. The second part of question is the location where you want to physically keep the backup media. It can be stored at same location (**onsite**) or at remote location (**offsite**). The benefit of storing at same location is easy and quick availability in case of loss of data but when there is total loss of site in case of flood , hurricane or fire ,offsite backup is more useful. According to the best practices, you should follow 3-2-1 plan. In this, you keep three backup copies of your data two copies onsite and third copy offsite. If condition arises, in which you require backup copy to restore data you have two good copies of data onsite and in case of total disaster, remote copy is there.

When

Next question, when to take backup? It all depends on your business needs. Frequency of data backup depends on frequency of change and criticality of data. Next thing, which define backup time, is functionality of system. System used for server and system used as workstation can have different backup windows.

Backup type

Now you know the answer of three W's, its time to understand backup more deeply. Backup is broadly of three types depending on how much backup you are taking.

1. Full backup
2. Differential backup
3. Incremental backup

Full backup

As name suggest it is backup which contains all files. When you require to restore only one full backup is required.

Differential backup

A differential backup is cumulative backup of files, which have changed since last full backup. In case of restore only last full backup and last differential backup is required.

Incremental backup

Incremental backup backs up only the changed data since the last backup, whether it is a full or incremental backup. Suppose you have taken full backup on Sunday. On Monday, you will take incremental backup of changed files since Sunday. On Tuesday if you take incremental backup once again, it will backup only files that has changed since last incremental backup i.e. since Monday. However, if you take differential backup on Tuesday it will take backup of all files that have changed since full backup i.e. Sunday.

Backup tools for CentOS Backup

CentOS provides some basic tools to take backup. If you require advanced features, you can use proprietary tools which provides automated backup, backup over network, backup using own database etc.

CentOS basic tools for full and partial backup are following

- Tar
- CPIO
- dump and restore

Advanced utility for CentOS backup

The **A**dvanced **M**aryland **A**utomatic **N**etwork **D**isk **A**rchiver (AMANDA) client/ server based utility which uses dump or tar to take backup over network.

Proprietary tools for backup

Some of the corporate tools for backup which are more advanced and feature rich :-

- IBM's Tivoli Storage Manager
- Veritas Netbackup
- EMC NetWorker
- HPE StoreOnce

CentOS backup tools explained

Tar

Tar is the most versatile tool in Unix and Linux to take backup. Tar command is use to create one archive file of multiple files. You can copy tar archive files to tape, DVD or USB drive as a backup. You can also create compressed file by adding options while creating achieve file.

<u>Create tar</u>

Syntax

```
tar cvf name_of_archive_file files_or_directory_to_archive
```

Where

c   create

v   verbose

f   file name types of achieve file

Example

```
# cd /var/log
# tar cvf /backup/varlogs.tar *.log
boot.log
vmware-vmsvc.log
vmware-vmusr.log
wpa_supplicant.log
Xorg.0.log
Xorg.1.log
Xorg.9.log
yum.log
# ls -la /backup
total 144
drwxr-xr-x.  2 root root     25 Mar  8 04:11 .
dr-xr-xr-x. 21 root root   4096 Mar  8 04:07 ..
-rw-r--r--.  1 root root 143360 Mar  8 04:11 varlogs.tar
```

Create compressed tar file

You can compress the archive backup using tar options. Tar provides two type of compression gzip and bzip.

Create gzip format tar file

Syntax

```
# tar cvfz nameoftarfile.tar.gz name_of_files
```

Example

```
# tar cvfz /backup/varlogs.tar.gz *.log
```

Create bzip format

Syntax

```
# tar cvfj nameoftarfile.tar.bz2 name_of_files
```

Example

```
# tar cvfj /backup/varlogs.tar.bz2 *.log
```

Extract

To restore the files taken backup with tar command

```
# tar xvf /backup/varlogs.tar
```

Where

x   extract

v   verbose

f   file name types of achieve file

gzip format

Syntax

```
tar xvfz filename
```

Example

```
# tar xvfz /backup/varlogs.tar.gz
```

bzip format

Syntax

```
tar xvfj filename
```

Example

```
# tar xvfj /backup/varlogs.tar.bz2
```

List

Use **t** option to show content of archive file. Same command can be used to list the content of compressed files

List the archived tar file

Syntax

```
tar tvf filename
```

Example

```
# tar tvf /backup/varlogs.tar
# tar tvf /backup/varlogs.tar.bz2
# tar tvf /backup/varlogs.tar.gz
```

CPIO

CPIO utility copies files from and to achieve. It can be used for achieving and for copping files from one place to another.

To archive all files in **/var/log** folder to **backup** folder

```
# cd /var/log
```

```
# ls |cpio -ov > /backup/varlogs.cpio
```

To extract files from CPIO backup

```
# mkdir newbackup
# cd newbackup
# cpio -idv < /backup/varlogs.cpio
```

Creating archive from list of specific files.

Example :- archive all files with log extension from **var** directory

```
# find /var -iname *.log -print|cpio -ov > /backup/varlog.cpio
```

CPIO to create tar file

```
# ls|cpio -ovH tar -F abc.tar
```

To extract tar file using CPIO

```
# cpio -idv -F abc.tar
```

dump and restore

xfsdump

xfsdump utility is used to take backup of whole file system or files that has changed since last dump. Ideally, dump should be taken on the quiescent file system, so that files should not change during backup.

Syntax

```
xfsdump <options> target_device  filessystem_tobe backed_up
```

Example

To take backup of whole root filesystem to device st0

```
# xfsdump -l 0 -f /dev/st0 /
```

Where

-l   for dumpl level . There are ten dump levels from **0 to 9**

      0   complete

      1   increment from last backup

      2-9   increment from last incremental backup

-f   for device name

xfsrestore

xfsrestore command is used to restore the backup taken with dump command

Syntax

```
xfsrestore <options> backupdevice target
```

Example

To restore backup stored on /dev/st0 device

```
# xfsrestore -f /dev/st0 /home1
```

where option

-f   is for device name

## Chapter 15

Archiving and Compression

Archiving is the process of collecting and storing a group of files and directories into one file, Tar, cpio, zip and ar are example of utilities which performs this action. Whereas compression is processes of reducing the size of files using mathematical compression algorithm. It is quite useful in sending large files over the internet. Example of compression utilities are gzip, bzip2, xz etc.

GZIP

With gzip you can compress and decompress individual file. When you give gzip command to compress any file, the file will be replaced with extension .gz file keeping the same ownership modes, access and modification times. In sort, you will not see original file only compressed file will be there.

Syntax

```
gzip filename
```

Example

```
gzip sysctl.conf
```

Decompress

To decompress the compressed file use gunzip command. However this command will remove the compressed file you will see only uncompressed file only.

Syntax

```
gunzip filename
```

Example

```
gunzip sysctl.conf.gz
```

BZIP2

Bzip compresses file using compression algorithm known as Burrows Wheel block sorting. Like gzip it removes the original file and creates compressed file with same name plus extension bz2. Each compressed file has same modification date, permission and if possible with same ownership as corresponding original file.

Syntax

```
bzip2 filename
```

Example

```
bzip2 sysctl.conf
```

Decompress

To decompress the file compressed with bzip2 command use bunzip2. By default it will not overwrite if file of same name exist unless you give –f option

Syntax

```
bunzip2 filename
```

Example

```
bunzip2 sysctl.conf.bz2
```

XZ

xz is successor of the lzma utility, it will add .xz extension to compressed file automatically and remove original file. Like bzip and gzip it will keep same modification date, permission and if possible with same ownership as corresponding original file.

Syntax

```
xz filename
```

Example

```
xz sysctl.conf
```

Decompress

Syntax

```
unxz filename
```

Example

```
unxz sysctl.conf.xz
```

ZIP

Zip is archiving and compression utility. It creates files with .zip extension. It is cross platform compression utility so you can compress and decompress files from Linux to windows or vice versa. It will keep the original files intact

Syntax

```
zip zipfile.zip file/files_to_compress
```

Example

```
zip abc.zip sysctl.conf signond.conf
```

you can use zip also with wild cards

```
zip abc.zip s*
```

Zip files recursively (include sub directories also)

Syntax

```
zip -r zipfile.zip directoryname
```

Example

```
zip -r asp.zip monk
```

Listing content of compressed file

Syntax

```
unzip -l zipfile.zip
```

Example

```
unzip -l asp.zip
```

Decompress

To decompress compressed files with zip command unzip is used

Syntax

```
unzip zipfile.zip
```

Example

```
unzip asp.zip
```

ar

ar is not so known predecessor of rar which is in still in use in CentOS. It used for archiving only as such there is no compression in it.

Create archive

Syntax

```
ar cvsr archivefile.a files_to_archive
```

Example

```
ar cvsr abc.a s*
```

Extract archive

Syntax

```
ar xv archivefile.a
```

Example

```
ar xv abc.a
```

There are many third party utilities available which can be installed, you can try following

- peazip
- p7zip
- pax
- kgb

Many more..

## Chapter 16

Firewall

According to dictionary, a firewall is a wall or partition designed to inhibit or prevent the spread of fire. In computer world, firewall is network security system used to secure the incoming and outgoing connections. It prevents unauthorized access to the system. It restricts user to access only designated services.

Firewalld

Firewalld is the new interface in CentOS 7. It replaces the **iptables** interface and connects to the netfilter kernel code. FirewallD uses services and zones instead of iptables rules and chains. firewalld stores its rules in various XML files under **/usr/lib/firewalld/** and **/etc/firewalld/** folders. Firewalld allows security configuration without stopping current configuration. In earlier version with **iptables** every change requires flushing of all old rules and reading new rules from iptable configuration file, but in firewalld only new differences are applied without disturbing current connections.

A command-line client **firewall-cmd**, is provided. It can be used to make permanent and runtime changes to firewall rules. You require be root or administrative privileges to run **firewalld-cmd** command

Install firewalld

```
yum install firewalld
```

Check the status

```
systemctl status firewalld
```

or

```
firewall-cmd --state
```

Firewalld concepts

Configuration options

Rules of firewalld can be designated as either permanent or Runtime. Runtime changes are those changes to firewall settings that take effect immediately but are not permanent. Runtime changes will not retain after reboot of system or configuration reload. Whereas permanent changes are those changes which are written into configuration files but will not be applied immediately unless you reload the configuration or reboot the machine.

Zones

In firewalld concept of zone is based on network interface. All network interfaces can be located in the same default zone or divided into different zones according to the levels of trust defined. By defualt public zone is used for configuration. If you have more than one interface than you can create more zones and restrict trafic between zones. Lets take example if we have web server having two interface one connecting to outside world i.e. public zone and second interface in trusted zone that connects to database server.

Note: Without any configuration, everything is done by default in the public zone.

List of zones with explanation

- **Drop**

  Drop all incoming connections, only outgoing network connections are available.

- **Block**

  Allows only outgoing network connection. Reject all incoming connection with icmp-host-prohibited message.

- **Public**

  You do not trust the other computers on the network. Only selected incoming connections are accepted. For use in public areas.

- **Home**

  Only selected incoming connections are accepted. For use in home area

- **Work**

  You mostly trust the other computers on networks. Only selected incoming connections are accepted. For use in work areas.

- **Dmz**

  For the computers in DMZ demilitarized zone that are publicly accessible with limited access to the internal network, only selected incoming connections are accepted.

- **External**

  For use on external networks with masquerading enabled. Only selected incoming connections are accepted.

- **Internal**

  For use on internal networks. You mostly trust the other computers on the networks. Only selected incoming connections are accepted.

- **Trusted**

  All network connections are accepted.

Zones commands

List the available zones

```
# firewall-cmd --get-zones
```

To display default zone

```
# firewall-cmd --get-default-zone
```

Change the default zone

```
# firewall-cmd --set-default-zone= internal
```

Check the zone interface is associated with

```
# firewall-cmd --get-zone-of-interface=ens33
```

Change the zone of the interface

```
# firewall-cmd --permanent --zone=internal --change-interface=
ens33
```

Services

Firewalld services allows network traffic based on predefined rules. A Firewalld service can be a list of local ports, protocols and destinations.

You can also create your own custom rules for services. The **/usr/lib/firewalld/services** directory contains configuration files for default supported services and custom service files created by users are located in **/etc/firewalld/services** directory.

List of services in the default zone

```
# firewall-cmd --list-services
```

Add a service permanently to default zone
Syntax

```
# firewall-cmd --permanent --add-service=servicename
```

Example

```
# firewall-cmd --permanent --add-service=http
```

After that, you have to reload the new configuration

```
# firewall-cmd --reload
```

Add service to specific zone

```
# firewall-cmd --permanent --zone=internal --add-service=http
```

Port

Firewalld allows us to manage the network port directly.

List of ports in the default zone

```
# firewall-cmd --list-ports
```

Opening Port in the Firewall

To open up a new port (e.g., TCP/5903) permanently, use these commands.

```
# firewall-cmd --permanent --zone=public --add-port=5903/tcp
```

Then reload the configuration

```
# firewall-cmd --reload
```

Check the new configuration

```
# firewall-cmd --list-ports
```

Firewall configuration using GUI

If you do not like to use commands, CentOS 7 also provides GUI interface for configuration of firewall.

Installation

If GUI firewall is not already installed it can be installed with following command

```
# yum install system-config-firewall
```

There are two version of firewall interface, the first one is a version that runs under Gnome, and second one works on the command line. Here we will discuss Gnome version.

To start the GUI login as root on Gnome terminal

Run terminal window

In the terminal windows write following command

```
# firewall-config
```

Or you can click Application > sundry > firewall in GNOME classic mode

It will open firewall interface

Changing the Firewall Settings

Changing Configuration

When you start the interface, **Runtime** configuration is selected from the configuration dropdown menu for immediate change in the current firewall settings, Alternatively to apply the setting on next system start or firewall configuration reload , select Permanent from the drop-down list.

Change zone of Connection

To configure or add connection to a zone start firewall-config , from the option menu select **Change zone of connections**. It will show sub

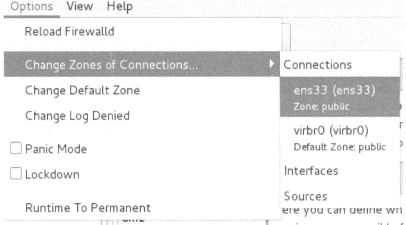

menu with list of connections available, select the desired connection from the dropdown menu. From next dropdown menu, select the Zone.

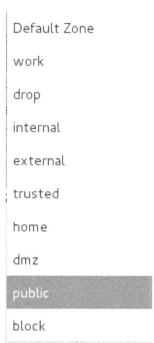

Set default zone

To set the default zone for new interface or change the default zone for a existing interface, start **firewall-config**, First select the desired connection then select Options from the menu bar, and select **Change Default Zone** from the drop-down menu. Now select the require zone from the list Menu.

Select zone for connec...

Select zone for
connection 'ens33'

public ▼

Close   OK

Configuring services

Firewall-config tool provides interface to enable and disable predefined or custom services. First, select the zone whose service you want to configure. Next is to select or deselect the service check box. Selected

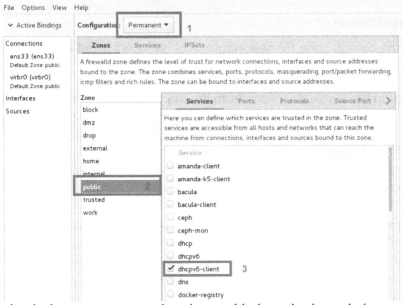

check box means service is enabled and cleared (un-selected) checkbox is to block the service.

To Enable/ disable a service, start the firewall-config tool and select Permanent/Runtime mode from the **Configuration** drop-down. Select the service you want to configure.

## Chapter 17

Partition and file system

Hard disk or hard drive is piece of hardware installed in your PC or server that stores data and provides quick access to large amounts of data on an electromagnetically charged surface or set of chips. Today capacity of hard disk can be in gigabytes and terabytes of storage. Hard disk can be attached internally or externally. With ever increasing capacity of hard disk you are tempted to install more than one Operating system on the same machine for that you do partitioning of hard disk. Partitioning also can be used to keep Operating system, application and data separate for better storage management.

Partitions

Partition in computer language is to divide the storage, mostly hard disk into segments in which you can have more than one file systems. Partitioning of storage helps in better storage management and easy backup. There are variety of tools available in Linux for storage partition like fdisk, Gnome disks and Parted etc. We will discuss two main tools fdisk and parted in this chapter.

Fdisk

fdisk is a powerful and most popular command line tool used for partition management. It is a text based menu-driven program for creation and manipulation of partition tables. It supports multiple types of partition tables formats, including MS-DOS and GPT. It provides interface to display, create, resize, delete and modify partitions on disks.

Fdisk for partition management

List the partition table

```
fdisk -l
```

List the partition table for specific

Syntax

```
fdisk -l <device name >
```

Example

```
fdisk -l /dev/hda1
```

Create new partition on device

In this example /dev/sdb is added to system

1. First print the list of all storage devices and check the device name for the device on which you want to create partition

```
# fdisk -l
Disk /dev/sdb: 21.5 GB, 21474836480 bytes
255 heads, 63 sectors/track, 2610 cylinders
Units = cylinders of 16065 * 512 = 8225280 bytes
Sector size (logical/physical): 512 bytes / 512 bytes
----Output is truncated -----
```

It will show the all storage device

2. Run fdisk on required device

```
# fdisk -cu /dev/sdb
```

3. Print the partition table of selected device

Press **p** and **enter** key

```
Command (m for help): p


Disk /dev/sdb: 21.5 GB, 21474836480 bytes
255 heads, 63 sectors/track, 2610 cylinders, total 41943040
sectors
Units = sectors of 1 * 512 = 512 bytes
Sector size (logical/physical): 512 bytes / 512 bytes
I/O size (minimum/optimal): 512 bytes / 512 bytes
Disk identifier: 0xdec2ee90


   Device Boot       Start         End      Blocks   Id  System
```
Output shows no partition present on sdb device

4. Press **n** to create new partition

```
Command (m for help): n
```

5. Press **p** to set partition type as primary or Press **e** for extended
   partition

```
Command action
   e   extended
   p   primary partition (1-4)
p
```

6. Give partition number like **1, 2, 3, 4.** If it is first partition on this
   device then press 1 for second partition press 2 like that

```
Partition number (1-4): 1
```

7. Press enter to use default starting sector or you can enter desired value if you do not want to start from the default sector

```
First sector (2048-41943039, default 2048):
Using default value 2048
```

8. For last sector, if you can calculate the size with sector numbers you can give sector number, otherwise you can give size like +1G to create 1 GB partition. If you press **Enter** without any value it will create partition on whole remaining space on the device

```
Last sector, +sectors or +size{K,M,G} (2048-41943039, default
41943039): +1G
```

9. Press **w** to write on disk

Delete the partition

To delete partition present on disk drive using fdisk following procedure is there. In this example device name /dev/sdb and we want to delete the /dev/sdb2 partition.

Display partition table of the desired device

```
[root@centos2 ~]# fdisk -l /dev/sdb

Disk /dev/sdb: 21.5 GB, 21474836480 bytes, 41943040 sectors
Units = sectors of 1 * 512 = 512 bytes
Sector size (logical/physical): 512 bytes / 512 bytes
I/O size (minimum/optimal): 512 bytes / 512 bytes
Disk label type: dos
Disk identifier: 0xd397c54b
```

Device Boot	Start	End	Blocks	Id	System
/dev/sdb1	2048	1955839	976896	83	Linux
/dev/sdb2	**1955840**	**41943039**	**19993600**	**83**	**Linux**

Once you know the device partition number to delete give disk command with device name

```
[root@centos2 ~]# fdisk /dev/sdb
Welcome to fdisk (util-linux 2.23.2).


Changes will remain in memory only, until you decide to write them.
Be careful before using the write command.


Command (m for help):
```

Press '**d**' to delete the partition

```
Command (m for help): d
```

Give the partition number to delete in this case partition number is 2 . press 2 and press **Enter**.

```
Partition number (1,2, default 2): 2
Partition 2 is deleted
```

Print the new partition table by pressing p and **Enter**

```
Command (m for help): p

Disk /dev/sdb: 21.5 GB, 21474836480 bytes, 41943040 sectors
Units = sectors of 1 * 512 = 512 bytes
Sector size (logical/physical): 512 bytes / 512 bytes
I/O size (minimum/optimal): 512 bytes / 512 bytes
```

```
Disk label type: dos
Disk identifier: 0xd397c54b


    Device Boot      Start         End      Blocks   Id  System
/dev/sdb1            2048     1955839       976896   83  Linux
```

Write the changes by pressing **w** key. If you quite without writing all changes will lost as all these changes are still in memory.

```
Command (m for help): w
The partition table has been altered!
Calling ioctl() to re-read partition table.
Syncing disks.
```

Alter partition

You can use fdisk to alter partition. In this example we will change the partition type from Linux to Linux LVM

1. First view the current partition table to selected device

```
[root@centos2 ~]# fdisk -l /dev/sdb


Disk /dev/sdb: 21.5 GB, 21474836480 bytes, 41943040 sectors
Units = sectors of 1 * 512 = 512 bytes
Sector size (logical/physical): 512 bytes / 512 bytes
I/O size (minimum/optimal): 512 bytes / 512 bytes
Disk label type: dos
Disk identifier: 0xd397c54b


    Device Boot      Start         End      Blocks   Id  System
/dev/sdb1            2048     2099199      1048576   83  Linux
/dev/sdb2         2099200    41943039     19921920   83  Linux
```

133

Now run fdisk with device name

```
[root@centos2 ~]# fdisk /dev/sdb
Welcome to fdisk (util-linux 2.23.2).


Changes will remain in memory only, until you decide to write
them.
Be careful before using the write command.
To change partition type
Command (m for help): t
Partition number (1,2, default 2): 1
Hex code (type L to list all codes): L


0   Empty            24  NEC DOS         81  Minix / old Lin bf  Solaris
1   FAT12            27  Hidden NTFS Win 82  Linux swap / So c1  DRDOS/sec
(FAT-
2   XENIX root       39  Plan 9          83  Linux           c4  DRDOS/sec
(FAT-
3   XENIX usr        3c  PartitionMagic  84  OS/2 hidden C:  c6  DRDOS/sec
(FAT-
4   FAT16 <32M       40  Venix 80286     85  Linux extended  c7  Syrinx
5   Extended         41  PPC PReP Boot   86  NTFS volume set da  Non-FS data
6   FAT16            42  SFS             87  NTFS volume set db  CP/M / CTOS /
.
7   HPFS/NTFS/exFAT  4d  QNX4.x          88  Linux plaintext de  Dell Utility
8   AIX              4e  QNX4.x 2nd part 8e  Linux LVM       df  BootIt
9   AIX bootable     4f  QNX4.x 3rd part 93  Amoeba          e1  DOS access
a   OS/2 Boot Manag  50  OnTrack DM      94  Amoeba BBT      e3  DOS R/O
b   W95 FAT32        51  OnTrack DM6 Aux 9f  BSD/OS          e4  SpeedStor
c   W95 FAT32 (LBA)  52  CP/M            a0  IBM Thinkpad hi eb  BeOS fs
e   W95 FAT16 (LBA)  53  OnTrack DM6 Aux a5  FreeBSD         ee  GPT
f   W95 Ext'd (LBA)  54  OnTrackDM6      a6  OpenBSD         ef  EFI (FAT-
12/16/
10  OPUS             55  EZ-Drive        a7  NeXTSTEP        f0  Linux/PA-RISC
b
11  Hidden FAT12     56  Golden Bow      a8  Darwin UFS      f1  SpeedStor
```

```
12  Compaq diagnost 5c  Priam Edisk      a9  NetBSD          f4  SpeedStor
14  Hidden FAT16 <3 61  SpeedStor        ab  Darwin boot     f2  DOS secondary
16  Hidden FAT16    63  GNU HURD or Sys  af  HFS / HFS+      fb  VMware VMFS
17  Hidden HPFS/NTF 64  Novell Netware   b7  BSDI fs         fc  VMware
VMKCORE
18  AST SmartSleep  65  Novell Netware   b8  BSDI swap       fd  Linux raid
auto
1b  Hidden W95 FAT3 70  DiskSecure Mult  bb  Boot Wizard hid fe  LANstep
1c  Hidden W95 FAT3 75  PC/IX            be  Solaris boot    ff  BBT
1e  Hidden W95 FAT1 80  Old Minix
Hex code (type L to list all codes): 8e
Changed type of partition 'Linux' to 'Linux LVM'


Command (m for help): w
The partition table has been altered!


Calling ioctl() to re-read partition table.
Syncing disks.
```

Now list the partition to verify

```
[root@centos2 ~]# fdisk -l /dev/sdb


Disk /dev/sdb: 21.5 GB, 21474836480 bytes, 41943040 sectors
Units = sectors of 1 * 512 = 512 bytes
Sector size (logical/physical): 512 bytes / 512 bytes
I/O size (minimum/optimal): 512 bytes / 512 bytes
Disk label type: dos
Disk identifier: 0xd397c54b


Device Boot      Start         End      Blocks   Id  System
/dev/sdb1         2048     2099199     1048576   8e  Linux LVM
/dev/sdb2      2099200    41943039    19921920   83  Linux
```

Parted

Parted is a famous command line tool that allows you to easily manage hard disk partitions. The utility parted allows users to:

- View the existing partition table
- Add partitions from free space or additional hard drives
- Delete existing partitions

Install Parted on Linux

If parted is not installed on your Linux machine you can install it using following command

```
# yum install parted
```

Check version of installed parted

To know version of installed parted either you can give parted -v

```
[root@centos2 ~]# parted -v
parted (GNU parted) 3.1
Copyright (C) 2012 Free Software Foundation, Inc.
License GPLv3+: GNU GPL version 3 or later
<http://gnu.org/licenses/gpl.html>.
This is free software: you are free to change and redistribute
it.
There is NO WARRANTY, to the extent permitted by law.
```

List partitions

To list partition start parted and give print command or

parted -l

```
[root@centos2 ~]# parted -l
```

```
Model: VMware, VMware Virtual S (scsi)
Disk /dev/sda: 21.5GB
Sector size (logical/physical): 512B/512B
Partition Table: msdos
Disk Flags:

Number  Start   End     Size    Type     File system   Flags
 1      1049kB  10.7GB  10.7GB  primary  xfs           boot
 2      10.7GB  15.0GB  4295MB  primary  linux-swap(v1)

<output truncated >
```

List Partition of specific disk

To list partition of specific disk, give parted command with device name then `print` and `quit` command

```
[root@centos2 ~]# parted /dev/sda
GNU Parted 3.1
Using /dev/sda
Welcome to GNU Parted! Type 'help' to view a list of commands.
(parted) print
Model: VMware, VMware Virtual S (scsi)
Disk /dev/sda: 21.5GB
Sector size (logical/physical): 512B/512B
Partition Table: msdos
Disk Flags:

Number  Start   End     Size    Type     File system   Flags
 1      1049kB  10.7GB  10.7GB  primary  xfs           boot
 2      10.7GB  15.0GB  4295MB  primary  linux-swap(v1)
(parted) quit
```

Create partition

If you have added new disk to system and want to add partition table to it, first decide which type of partition you have two options it can be either MBR or GPT. Use mklabel command with partition type, for MBR type partition write msdos for GPT type partition write gtp.

```
[root@centos2 ~]# parted /dev/sdb
GNU Parted 3.1
Using /dev/sdb
Welcome to GNU Parted! Type 'help' to view a list of commands.
(parted) mklabel msdos
Warning: The existing disk label on /dev/sdb will be destroyed
and all data on this disk will be lost. Do you want to
continue?
Yes/No? yes
(parted)
```

Following are the steps to add a partition
1. Give **parted** command with required device name
2. use **mkpart** command
3. Select partition type, it can be **primary or extended**
4. Give file system type default is **ext2**
5. Like fdisk give starting and ending sector number if disk is new starting sector will be 1 and for ending you can give size like 1G for 1GB partition size

```
(parted) mkpart
Partition type?  primary/extended? primary
File system type?  [ext2]?
Start? 1
```

```
End? 1G
(parted) print
Model: VMware, VMware Virtual S (scsi)
Disk /dev/sdb: 21.5GB
Sector size (logical/physical): 512B/512B
Partition Table: msdos
Disk Flags:

Number  Start   End     Size    Type      File system  Flags
 1      1049kB  1000MB  999MB   primary
(parted) quite
```

Add partition

If you have space available on the hard disk and you want to add one more partition you can give **mkpart** command in parted interface. It will ask same question as in case of creating first partition. However, this time start will be end of the previous partition. Start of this partition plus size of the partition is the **end** of the partition. In this example, start is 1000MB as the end is at 1000MB for first partition and end of this partition will be 2000MB(1000MB + 1000MB) if you want add 1000MB partition.

```
(parted) mkpart
Partition type?  primary/extended? primary
File system type?  [ext2]?
Start? 1000MB
End? 2000MB
(parted) print
Model: VMware, VMware Virtual S (scsi)
Disk /dev/sdb: 21.5GB
```

139

```
Sector size (logical/physical): 512B/512B
Partition Table: msdos
Disk Flags:


Number  Start    End      Size    Type      File system  Flags
 1       1049kB   1000MB   999MB   primary
 2       1000MB   2000MB   999MB   primary
```

Delete partition

To delete the partition use `rm partition_number` command.

Example

```
 (parted) print
Model: VMware, VMware Virtual S (scsi)
Disk /dev/sdb: 21.5GB
Sector size (logical/physical): 512B/512B
Partition Table: msdos
Disk Flags:


Number  Start    End      Size     Type      File system  Flags
 1       1049kB   1000MB   999MB    primary
 2       1001MB   2001MB   999MB    primary
 3       2001MB   3001MB   1000MB   primary


(parted) rm 3
(parted) print
Model: VMware, VMware Virtual S (scsi)
Disk /dev/sdb: 21.5GB
Sector size (logical/physical): 512B/512B
Partition Table: msdos
Disk Flags:
```

```
Number  Start   End     Size    Type     File system  Flags
1       1049kB  1000MB  999MB   primary
2       1001MB  2001MB  999MB   primary
```

In this Chapter, we learned how to manage partitions, in the next chapter we will discuss how to create filesystem on these partitions.

Chapter 18.

File system

File System is method used by operating system to store and retrieve data. File system helps in managing and arranging data. There are different types of file systems available in Linux. Each type of file system uses different structure and logic for storing and retrieving data. Some file systems have been specifically designed for specific devices and applications, for example ISO 9660 file system is used for optical disks like CDROM. Depending of file system type it can be local or over network. Linux support wide variety of file systems each file system has pros and cons. We will discuss some of the common filesystems used in CentOS.

XFS

XFS is a high-performance journaling file system that was initially created by Silicon Graphics, Inc. for the IRIX operating system and later ported to Linux. XFS supports metadata journaling, which facilitates quicker crash recovery. The XFS file system can also be defragmented and enlarged while mounted and active. XFS records file system updates asynchronously to a circular buffer (the journal) before it can commit the actual data updates to disk. XFS is default File system for CentOS 7

Creating XFS file system

1. Create partition using fdisk as described in the earlier chapter
2. **fdisk -l** check the required device name

3. **mkfs -t xfs /dev/sdb1** where **sdb1** is device name and **xfs** is file system type.

```
~]# mkfs -t xfs /dev/sdb1
```

4. **create mount point**

```
~]# mkdir /test1
```

5. **Add entry in the /etc/fstab**

```
~]# vi /etc/fstab
/dev/mapper/cl-root /      xfs      defaults        1 1
UUID=6b761a5f-8c7c-465d-b58c-d29267938403 /boot  xfs defaults          1 2
/dev/mapper/cl-swap swap swap     defaults         0 0
/dev/sdb1         /test1         xfs      defaults         0 2
```

Where **/dev/sdb1** is device   **/test1** mount point, **xfs** for partition type, 0 for dump and 2 order for fsck.

EXT File System

Extended file system (EXT) is most popular file system used in Linux Operating systems. In its lifespan it had evolved a lot from its first implementation in 1992 to till date. EXT 4 is the most recent version of EXT. From third generation i.e. **EXT 3** it came up with journalized file system. With JFS feature it keep the track of changes not yet committed to the file system by recording such changes in data structure to journal which in turn generate circular log. In case of abrupt system down like power failure or crashed file system can be brought back online easily. **EXT3** having limitation of file system size as 8TB /16TB and file size as 2 TB whereas **Ext4** is the next generation of ext file system having

143

improved file system and file size upper limits of 16TB. It is efficient reliable and robust. Ext4 is a deeper improvement over Ext3.

Creating EXT4 file system

1. Create partition with fdisk
2. **fdisk -l** check the device name
3. **mkfs -t ext4 /dev/sdb1** where **sdb1** is device name and **ext4** is file system type

Syntax

```
mkfs -t ext4 device_name
```

Example

```
~]# mkfs -t ext4 /dev/sdb1
```

Or

```
~]# mkfs.ext4 /dev/sdb1
```

4. **create mount point**

```
~]# mkdir /test1
```

5. **Mount new File system**

```
~]# mount -t ext4 /dev/sdb1 /test1
```

6. **Add entry in the /etc/fstab**

```
~]# vi /etc/fstab
/dev/mapper/cl-root /      xfs      defaults      1 1
UUID=6b761a5f-8c7c-465d-b58c-d29267938403 /boot  xfs defaults      1 2
/dev/mapper/cl-swap swap swap      defaults      0 0
/dev/sdb1        /test1          ext4      defaults      0 2
```

Btrfs (Technology Preview)

CentOS 7 introduces btrfs as a Technology Preview. Btrfs (B-tree file system) is new file system introduced as technology preview in CentOS 7 version. It is next generation file system, which offers features like more scalability, self-healing and better management. Not only that It also offers snapshot, file striping and compression capabilities.

```
[root@centos1 ~]# mkfs.btrfs /dev/sdb1
btrfs-progs v4.4.1
See http://btrfs.wiki.kernel.org for more information.


Label:              (null)
UUID:               3ce8cf05-3788-4424-b73f-2219b1e8e25b
Node size:          16384
Sector size:        4096
Filesystem size:    1.00GiB
Block group profiles:
  Data:             single            8.00MiB
  Metadata:         DUP               59.19MiB
  System:           DUP               12.00MiB
SSD detected:       no
Incompat features:  extref, skinny-metadata
Number of devices:  1
Devices:
   ID        SIZE  PATH
    1      1.00GiB  /dev/sdb1


[root@centos1 ~]# mkdir /test1
[root@centos1 ~]# mount /dev/sdb1 /test1
```

## Chapter 19

Swap space

Swap space is used in Linux and UNIX to free up physical memory. The inactive pages of data is written to slower storage i.e. hard disk. The area where inactive data is written is called as swap space.

Add swap space

1. Create partition

```
~]# fdisk /dev/sdb

WARNING: DOS-compatible mode is deprecated. It's strongly
recommended to switch off the mode (command 'c') and change
display units to sectors (command 'u').

Command (m for help): n
Command action
    e    extended
    p    primary partition (1-4)
p
Partition number (1-4): 2
First cylinder (307-6132, default 307):
Using default value 307
Last cylinder, +cylinders or +size{K,M,G} (307-6132, default
6132): +1G
```

Change the type by pressing **t** of partition selected to **82** which is Linux swap

```
Command (m for help): t
Partition number (1-4): 2
Hex code (type L to list codes): 82
Changed system type of partition 2 to 82 (Linux swap /
Solaris)


Check the partition
Command (m for help): p


Disk /dev/sdb: 21.5 GB, 21474836480 bytes
171 heads, 40 sectors/track, 6132 cylinders
Units = cylinders of 6840 * 512 = 3502080 bytes
Sector size (logical/physical): 512 bytes / 512 bytes
I/O size (minimum/optimal): 512 bytes / 512 bytes
Disk identifier: 0xdec2ee90


Device Boot    Start   End      Blocks    Id  System
/dev/sdb1         1     307     1048576   83  Linux
/dev/sdb2        307     614     1050280   82  Linux swap /
Solaris


Press w to write partition to disk
Command (m for help): w
The partition table has been altered!

Calling ioctl() to re-read partition table.
Syncing disks.
```

2. **mkswap /dev/sdb2** where sdb2 is name of the partition which will be used as swap.

```
~]# mkswap /dev/sdb2
Setting up swapspace version 1, size = 1050276 KiB
no label, UUID=c1f98067-9548-4bf1-843d-5f09f5d5ba56
```

3. Add entry in /etc/fstab

```
~]# cat /etc/fstab

/dev/mapper/cl-root /   xfs       defaults           1 1
UUID=6b761a5f-8c7c-465d-b58c-d29267938403 boot xfs
defaults        1 2
/dev/mapper/cl-swap swap                    swap    defaults
0 0
/dev/sdb1       /test1          xfs     defaults        0 2
UUID=c1f98067-9548-...5ba56 swap swap     defaults        0 0
```

4. swapon -a will activate swap

5. swapon -s will show status of all swap space

```
~]# swapon -s
Filename                Type            Size    Used
Priority
/dev/dm-1               partition       2097144 0           -1
/dev/sdb2               partition       1050272 0           -2
```

To deactivate the swap space

```
# swapoff /dev/sdb2
```

## Chapter 20

Logical Volume Manager

In earlier section we have learned about creating Linux partition but Linux provides option to create partition type as LVM (logical partition manager). LVM is more sophisticated than normal Linux partition. LVM offers following benefits

- Increase the File system dynamically
- Shrink the File system
- Add disk dynamically
- Mirroring
- Stripping
- Snapshot as backup of File system

Terms used in LVM

Physical Volume

Physical Volume (PV) is physical storage unit of an LVM is a block device such as a partition or whole disk. To use the device for an LVM create partition with **fdisk** as **LVM** type.

Volume Groups

One or more physical volumes combined into Volume Group (VG). Volume group is an abstract that presents underlying devices as a unified logical device with combined storage capacity of the physical volumes

Physical Extent

Storage space from Physical Volume is divided in to small unit of fixed size known as physical extent, which is smallest unit that can be allocated. P.E. size is always same for all physical volume in the same VG.

Logical extent

Mapping of PE to make up frontend of LVM. By default, one PE is generally mapped to one LE. However, you can map more than one PE to one LE in case of mirroring.

Logical Volume

Logical volume is group of Logical Extent. It is here we create File system. Logical volume is not restricted to physical disk sizes. In addition, the hardware storage layer is isolated from software.

Steps to create File system on new disk added to system

Create Physical volume (PV)

Use **fdisk** command and create partition type Linux LVM **8e**

```
~]# fdisk /dev/sdb


WARNING: DOS-compatible mode is deprecated. It's strongly
recommended to
        switch off the mode (command 'c') and change display
units to
        sectors (command 'u').
Command (m for help): n
```

```
Command action
   e   extended
   p   primary partition (1-4)
p
Partition number (1-4): 3
First cylinder (615-6132, default 615):
Using default value 615
Last cylinder, +cylinders or +size{K,M,G} (615-6132, default
6132): +5G

Command (m for help): t
Partition number (1-4): 3
Hex code (type L to list codes): 8e
Changed system type of partition 3 to 8e (Linux LVM)

Command (m for help): p

Disk /dev/sdb: 21.5 GB, 21474836480 bytes
171 heads, 40 sectors/track, 6132 cylinders
Units = cylinders of 6840 * 512 = 3502080 bytes
Sector size (logical/physical): 512 bytes / 512 bytes
I/O size (minimum/optimal): 512 bytes / 512 bytes
Disk identifier: 0xdec2ee90


Device Boot      Start        End       Blocks   Id  System
/dev/sdb1            1        307      1048576   83  Linux
/dev/sdb2          307        614      1050280   82  Linux swap
/ Solaris
/dev/sdb3          615       2148      5246280   8e  Linux LVM
```

```
Command (m for help): w
The partition table has been altered!
```

1. Reboot the server

2. Create PV using command **pvcreate** *device_name* where
   device_name is device created with fdisk

```
~]# pvcreate /dev/sdb3
    Physical volume "/dev/sdb3" successfully created
~]# pvdisplay /dev/sdb3
  "/dev/sdb3" is a new physical volume of "5.00 GiB"
  --- NEW Physical volume ---
  PV Name                /dev/sdb3
  VG Name
  PV Size                5.00 GiB
  Allocatable            NO
  PE Size                0
  Total PE               0
  Free PE                0
  Allocated PE           0
  PV UUID                EQ7ElZ-WiGK-Z0m5-5gSN-gP95-MFSk-pKyTvS
```

Defining Volume Group (VG)

vgcreate *VG_name PV_name*

```
~]# vgcreate vg01 /dev/sdb3
  Volume group "vg01" successfully created
```

Create new Logical Volume(LV)

```
lvcreate -n LV_name -L size VG_name
```

```
~]# lvcreate -n lv01 -L 1G vg01
  Logical volume "lv01" created
```

Create File System on LV

`mkfs -t xfs /dev/VG_name/LV_name` where **-t** option is to specify the file system type and logical volume name is specified in hierarchical order with respect to it volume group

```
~]# mkfs -t xfs /dev/vg01/lv01
```

Make New File system mount automatically

To make file system mount automatically at system boot you have to add its entry in /etc/fstab file. There are two ways to do that first is to use device name other is device Universally Unique Identifier UUID. The advantage of using the UUID is that it is independent from the actual device number the operating system gives your hard disk. Device name can change if you add new device, but device's UUID always remain same. To add it using UUID following are steps:-

1. Check the UUID of newly created file system

```
#  blkid /dev/vg01/lv01
```

2. Add entry to **/etc/fstab** mount system automatically at startup

```
UUID=6acaa-5541139e830e   /newfs    xfs    defaults        1 2
```

Mount the file system

```
mount -a
```

PV Commands

Description	Command
Display PV properties	pvdisplay
Show all LVM block devices	pvscan
Prevent allocation of PE on PV	pvchange -xn /dev/PV_name
Remove PV	pvremove /dev/PV_name

Volume Group Commands

Description	Command
Display VG properties	vgdisplay
Display VG List	vgs
Add PV to VG	vgextend vgname /dev/PV_name **Example** # vgextend vg01 /dev/sdb5
Remove PV from VG	vgreduce vg1 /dev/PV_name **Example** # vgreduce vg01 /dev/sdb5
Activating VG	vgchange -ay VG_name
deactivating VG	vgchange -ay VG_name
Remove VG	vgremove VG_name **Example** vgremove /dev/vg02
Recreate a VG Directory	vgmknodes

Moving Volume group

If situation arises, in which you have to move whole volume group from one system to other system. It can be due to some hardware problem on the current system or for moving old storage to new hardware you can use following procedure. In this example, there are two systems one is old system on which VG is currently located and new system that is where you want to move.

On old system

1. Unmount all File systems which are part of Volume Group

```
umount /newfs
```

2. Deactivate the VG **vgchange -an *VG_name*** command

```
[root@Centos1 /]# vgchange -an sharedvg
```

3. Export the VG with **vgexport *VG_name*** command

```
[root@centos1 /]# vgexport sharedvg
```

On New System

4. After attaching HDD to new system import the VG with **vgimport *VG_name*** command

```
[root@centos2 ~]# vgimport sharedvg
```

5. Activate the VG with **vgchange -ay VG_name**

```
[root@centos2 ~]# vgchange -ay sharedvg
```

6. Mount the file systems on the VG

```
[root@centos2 ~]# mount /dev/sharedvg/sharedlv /mnt
```

7. Check the contents of file system

```
[root@centos2 ~]# cd /mnt
```

Extending File System

1. Check the current FS size

```
df -h /fsname
```

```
/dev/mapper/vg01-lv01          1008M    34M   924M   4% /newfs
```

2. Check if you have enough free space i.e. free PE on the VG where
   LV of FS you want extend is there.

```
# vgdisplay vg01
  --- Volume group ---
  VG Name               vg01
  System ID
  Format                lvm2
  Metadata Areas        1
  Metadata Sequence No  5
  VG Access             read/write
  VG Status             resizable
  MAX LV                0
  Cur LV                1
  Open LV               1
  Max PV                0
  Cur PV                1
  Act PV                1
  VG Size               5.00 GiB
  PE Size               4.00 MiB
  Total PE              1280
  Alloc PE / Size       256 / 1.00 GiB
  Free  PE / Size       1024 / 4.00 GiB
  VG UUID               EXKfhW-MfE4-4ZtU-uQuM-v9e4-AJ9k-Uo6z4B
```

3. Extend the Logical Volume `lvextend -L size /dev/vgname/lvname`

```
# lvextend -L +200M /dev/vg01/lv01
   Extending logical volume lv01 to 1.20 GiB
   Logical volume lv01 successfully resized
```

4. Extend the file system using

```
xfs_growfs /fsname
```

```
# xfs_growfs /newfs
```

5. Check the FS size

```
df -h /fsname
```

```
/dev/mapper/vg01-lv01      1.2G   34M   1.1G   3% /newfs
```

Reduce the File System

1. Check the current FS size

```
df -h /fs_name
```

```
/dev/mapper/vg01-lv01      1.2G   34M   1.1G   3% /newfs
```

2. Backup the File System

```
# xfsdump -f /tmp/newfs.dump /newfs
```

3. unmount the Filesystem

```
umount /fs_name
```

```
# umount /newfs
```

4. Remove the LV

```
# lvremove /dev/mapper/vg01-lv01
```

5. Recreate LV

157

```
# lvcreate -n lv01 -L 1G vg01
```

6. Recreate the File system

```
# mkfs.xfs /dev/vg01/lv01
```

7. First check the UUID

```
# blkid /dev/vg01/lv01
```

8. Change the UUID of File system in /etc/fstab

9. Mount File System

```
# mount -a
```

10. Restore the backup

```
xfsrestore -f /tmp/newfs.dump /newfs
```

11. Check File System

```
# df -h /newfs
```

## Chapter 21

LVM snapshot

LVM snapshot is a point in time copy of Logical Volume. The snapshot provides static view of original volume. Once snapshot has been taken we can use this snapshot to take backup volume as snapshot is static copy and it will not change while backup is happening unlike the original volume which is dynamic.

The snapshot volume size should be enough to store the data that will change after snapshot has been taken. The volume will store only changes after the snapshot has been taken.

Create snapshot LV

1. Check the LV name and size of File System for which you want to create snapshot

```
# df -hT /newfs
Filesystem          Type  Size  Used Avail Use% Mounted on
/dev/mapper/vg01-lv01 ext4 1008M   34M  924M   4% /newfs
```

2. Check you have space at least equivalent to 10% of file system you want to take snapshot available on the VG where original LV is located

```
# vgdisplay vg01
```

3. Create LV 8 to 10 % of capacity of original LV

```
lvcreate -s -n snaplvname -L size /dev/vgname/orginal_lv_name
```

```
# lvcreate -s -n snaplv1 -L 100M /dev/mapper/vg01-lv01
```

4. if you want to see content of snapshot LV

```
mount -o ro /dev/vgname/snaplv /mount_point_snaplv
```

```
# mount -o ro /dev/vg01/snaplv1 /snapfs/
```

5. Change to directory to check the contents

```
cd /mount_point_snaplv
```

```
# cd /snapfs/
# ls
```

Remove snapshot LV

Once you have taken backup and you do not want this snapshot, you can remove it using following procedure

1. Unmount snap File system

```
umount /mount_point_snaplv
```

```
[root@centos1 /]# umount /snapfs
```

2. Remove the snap logical volume

```
lvremove /dev/vgname/snaplv
```

```
[root@Centos1 /]# lvremove /dev/mapper/vg01-snaplv1
```

## Chapter 22

Utilities and commands

In this chapter we will discuss some of the common command utilities very useful in CentOS administration. Most of the commands discussed in chapter can also be used on almost any flavor of Linux.

cp

Command to copy files

Syntax

```
cp <options> source destination
```

Example

```
cp /home/abc.txt /home1/
```

Copy all files in the directory recursively

```
cp -R   /home/* /home1/
```

Prompt before any overwrite

```
cp -i /home  /home1
```

Copy all new files to the destination

```
cp -u * /tmp
```

Forcefully copy files

```
cp -f /tmp/abc.txt /backup/.
```

Copy without prompting to overwrite

```
cp -n * t
```

scp

scp command is used to copy files from one host to another host in secured manner.

Copy files from local machine to remote machine

Syntax

```
scp filename remote_user@remote_host:/some/remote_diectory
```

Example

```
$ scp /home/ana/atom.txt adams@server1/home/adams/.
```

Copy files from remote host to local host

Syntax

```
scp remote_user@remote.host:/path/filename  .
```

Example

```
$ scp adams@server1/home/adams/tasks.txt /home/ana/.
```

ls

Lists the names of Files

Syntax

```
ls -<options>
```

Example

```
$ ls -al          To list directories and files
```

cat

Displays a Text File

Syntax

```
cat filename
```

Example

```
$ cat abc.conf
```

rm

Deletes a file, files or directory

Syntax

```
rm filename
```

Example

```
rm abc.conf
```

To delete abc directory recursively

```
rm -r abc
```

more

When you want to view a file that is longer than one screen, you can use more utility. More is used for paging through text one screen full at a time.

Syntax

```
more filename
```

Example

```
more /etc/hosts
```

less

Less is a program similar to more, but it allows backward movement in the file as well as forward movement.

Syntax

```
less filename
```

Example

```
less /etc/hosts
```

mv

mv command is used to move file from one location to other location. mv command can also be used to rename the file.

mv command to move file

Syntax

```
mv filename destination_directory
```

Example

```
mv a.txt /tmp/.
```

It will move a.txt file from current directory to /tmp directory

To rename

Syntax

```
mv filename newfilename
```

Example

```
mv a.txt b.txt
```

grep

Searches for a String from one or more files. Display each line which has string.

Syntax

```
grep string file
```

Example

```
grep '127.0.0.1' /etc/hosts
```

head

Print the first 10 lines of file to standard output. You can also specify how many line it will show.

Syntax

```
head option file
```

Example

```
head -20 /tmp/abc.txt
```

This command will show first 20 lines of abc.txt file

tail

Print the last 10 lines of file to standard output if used without any parameter, otherwise you can specify number of lines to display.

Syntax

```
tail option file
```

Example

```
tail -20 /var/log/logfile
```

It will show last 20 lines

Use tail to monitor file continuously

```
tail -f /var/log/logfile
```

It will show end of growing file. Press Ctrl +c to interrupt.

diff

Compares Two Files.

Syntax

```
diff First_file  Second_file
```

Example

```
diff abc.txt bbc.txt
```

file

Determine file type

Syntax

```
file file_name
```

Example

```
file bbc.txt
```

echo

Write arguments to the standard output

Syntax

```
echo text
```

Example

```
echo hello
```

date

Print or change the system data and time.

Syntax

```
date
```

Example

To check date

```
date
```

To set date

```
date -s "24 feb 2017 19:00"
```

## Chapter 23

Piping and Redirection

In the previous chapter we learned Linux commands in this chapter we will see how Linux commands and files can be used in conjunction with one another to turn simple commands into much more complex command. This involves movement of data from command to other command or command to file or file to command.

This data traveling from command to other command or file to command or file to command is known as stream. Stream can of three types:-

- Standard input (stdin)
- Standard output (stdout)
- Standard error (stderr)

Normally when user is working on a PC, standard input flows from keyboard of the user to standard out that is the monitor, where user see the output. If there are errors in the operation the user will see the standard error on the terminal. However, we can change this behavior by using angle brackets and pipes. Some time we refer these streams with their corresponding numbers.

Stream	Number	Sign	Append
Stdin	0	<	<<
stdout	1	>	>>
stderr	2	2>	2>>

Redirection

When you want change the normal flow of data we use redirection. You can send output of the command to file or device. You can also take input from file or device to command.

Sending output to file (>)

Normally, we get our output on the screen, but if we wish to save it into a file, then greater than operator (>) is used to send the standard out to file. Please note this command will overwrite content of the existing output file.

Syntax

```
Command > filename
```

Example

```
ls > abc.txt
```

Sending input from file (<)

If we use the less than operator (<) then we can read data from file and feed it into the program via it's STDIN stream.

Syntax

```
Command < filename
```

Example

```
wc -l < abc.txt
```

Sending standard error to file

If we use 2 with greater than operator (2>) then we can send STDERR stream to a file.

Syntax

```
Command or script 2> filename
```

Example

```
myscript 2>abc.log
```

Append

We have seen that use of the single-bracket command overwrites the prior contents of the file. To append the content we can use double brackets (>>) or (2>>)

To append the standard out to existing file or create new one if it is not there

Syntax

```
Command >> filename
```

Example

```
# la -la >> abc.txt
```

To append the stderr stream to file

Syntax

```
Command 2>> filename
```

Example

```
# myscript.sh 2>> abc.txt
```

Sometimes, you might want to redirect both standard output and standard error into same file. This is often done in case of automated processes so that you can review the output and errors if any, later. Use &> or &>> to redirect both standard output and standard error to the same place. Another way is to use the numbers of the stream 2>&1

Syntax
```
Command >outputfile 2>&1
```

Example
```
ls b* >abc.log 2>&1
```

Piping (|)

For sending data from one program to another, we use pipe (|)

Syntax
```
Command1 | Command2
```

Example
```
ls | head -10
```

This command run the ls command and shows only first 10 lines of the output. This is simple example of pipe to explain, but you can use pipe for more complex use.

First sort the abc.txt and then use uniq command print unique values.

```
$ sort abc.txt | uniq
```

## Chapter 24

Process and threads

Every task done by Linux OS has process associated with it. A tasks may consists of one or more processes. In the simplest terms, process is an executing program. Further process is executed in form of threads. A thread is the basic unit to which the operating system allocates processor time. The idea is to achieve parallelism by dividing a process into multiple threads. The primary difference between process and thread is that threads within the same process run in a shared memory space, while processes run in separate memory spaces. Processes have following properties: -

- Process has priority based on the context switches on them.
- Each process provide required resources to execute the program.
- Each process starts with single thread known as primary thread.
- Process can have multiple threads.
- Process runs in foreground and background

Foreground Processes
A foreground process is any command or task you run directly and wait for it to complete.

Background Process
Background process are process which runs behind the scene. Unlike with a foreground process, the shell does not have to wait for a background process to end before it can run more processes. The

maximum number of process that can run in background depends on amount of available memory.

Commands

Command	Description
bg	Sends job to Background
fg	Bring job to foreground
jobs	Show current jobs
kill	Stops the process
ps	Show the process information
&	if command ends with the & the shell execute the command in background and shell will not wait for finish Example gcalctool &

Bring command to foreground

```
$ fg
ctrl + c
```

Check the running jobs

$ jobs

List the current running process

```
$ ps -ef
```
or
```
$ ps aux
```

Kill the process forcefully

First check the process ID with **ps -ef** command then

```
$ sudo kill -9 <process -id >
```

Monitoring the process with ps command

ps command show the percentage of CPU & memory utilization of the process it is very useful if your machine is under performing. ps command gives you indication which process is hogging memory/CPU.

Process scheduling

Scheduler is part of kernel, which select process to run next. The purpose is to run the processes according to priorities. To set the priority of running process nice and renice command is used which decide how longer or smaller CPU time is given to process.

Nice   set the priority or niceness of new process.

renice   adjust nice value of running process

niceness of -20 is highest priority and 19 is lowest priority. The default priority is 0

Example
```
$ sudo nice -n 19 cp -r /as /map
```

Commands show priorities of running processes
```
ps -al
```
or
```
top
```

To change the priority

```
$ sudo renice -n 10 <pid>
```

Note: You need root / superuser privilege to change to higher priority.

## Chapter 25

Automating tasks

Automation of task is very important in computer field. Suppose you have to take daily backup at 11.00 O'clock in the night when there is no usage of system. Then you have to come in night to take backup. However, you can schedule your backup then computer will run the backup script at 11.00 o'clock in night automatically. In the morning you can verify the backup. CentOS provide many utilities to automate the task. These utilities can be used to automate the tasks which system administrators do regularly or at specified time. Following are the main utilities

- cron
- at
- batch

cron

cron is daemon that can be used to schedule the execution of recurring tasks according to time, day of month, day of week.

Configuration file

/etc/crontab

Command

Command	Description
crontab –l	List crontab entries
crontab –e	Edit crontab
crontab –r	Remove crontab

Format

minutes hours Day_of_month Month Day_of_week Command

Where

Minutes	(from 0 to 59)
hours	(from 0 to 23)
day of month	(from 1 to 31)
month	(from 1 to 12)
day of week	(from 0 to 6) (0=Sunday)

To schedule a recurring task

1. Edit crontab by giving command **crontab -e**

2. Add entries at bottom of file press **i**

Suppose you want to run backup script every night at 11:30

```
30      23 * * *       /myscripts/backup.sh
```

3. Press **ESCAPE** and press **:** write **x** after that press **ENTER** to save the entry .

at and batch

crontab is used for recurring task but for one time tasks at specified time at and batch commands are used.

To run **at** command rpm must be installed and **atd** service must be running. When you give at command with time, the system presents you the at prompt. On at prompt you can give the commands you want to schedule. After giving all commands, you press **CTRL + d** key to exit from at prompt.

Check Installation

```
# rpm -q at
```

Install at package

```
# yum install at
```

Start service

```
# service start atd
```

Start command

```
# at 4:00
at > ls
ctrl + d
```

Batch command executes one time task when system average load decreases bellow 0.8

```
~]# batch
at> ls -la
at> ctrl + d
```

Display list of pending jobs

```
# atq
```

## Chapter 26

Boot process

After pressing power on button to CentOS login prompt screen, system do lot of processing to get you to login prompt. This process is known as boot process. It is important to understand the boot process of Linux to troubleshoot startup issues and to configure Linux properly.

The following steps summarize how the boot procedure happens in CentOS

1. Computer uses **BIOS** to perform POST.
2. BIOS reads **Master Boot Record** for bootloader.
3. Control goes to **GRUB2**. It uses /boot/grub/grub.cfg to select the kernel image.
4. **Kernel**
   1. Mounts the **root filesystem** as specified with "root=" in grub.conf
   2. The kernel starts the **systemd** process with a process ID of 1 (PID 1)
   3. **initrd** which stands for Initial RAM Disk is used by kernel as temporary root file system until kernel is booted and the real root filesystem is mounted. It also contains drivers, which are required to access hard disk and other necessary hardware.

5. **systemd**
   Systemd is a system and service manager for Linux operating systems. It is designed to be backwards compatible with SysV

init scripts, and provides a number of features such as parallel startup of system services at boot time. systemd is the parent process of all processes on a system. systemd determine the default system target earlier it used to known as run level. After determining the target, it performs the initialization of system, which includes

1. Setting the host name
2. Initializing the network
3. Initializing the system hardware
4. Mounting the file systems
5. Starting swapping

## Chapter 27

Log management

Log files are very useful in troubleshooting the system. Log files are also usefull in auditing system for unauthorized system access. Log files give you an idea that what system was doing at specific point in time. Suppose your machine is running slow or not working properly as a Linux administrator, first thing to look for problem is logs. Logs provides clue when and how problem started and what part of OS is giving problem.

The log files generated in a Linux environment can normally be classified into four different categories:

- Application Logs
- Event Logs
- Service Logs
- System Logs

CentOS provide services for saving log information. Some application in CentOS use their own mechanism to logs directly to their log information files, example of which is apache Some of the service maintain their logs through systemctl. systemctl further communicates to Journald which keep track on log information.

Rsyslog is another logging method. Rsyslog and Journal, have several distinguishing features that make them suitable for specific use cases. In many situations, it is useful to combine their capabilities.

journald

journald daemon is a component of systemd which is used for logs managment. It's a centralized location for all messages logged by different components in a systemd enabled Linux system. This includes kernel and boot messages, initial RAM disk, messages coming from syslog or different services, it indexes and makes them available to the user. Log data collected by the journal is primarily text-based but can also include binary data where necessary. Log files produced by journald are not persistent, log files are stored only in memory or a small ring-buffer in the /run/log/journal/ directory. The amount of logged data depends on free memory. Logs gets rotated periodically. But you can configure the system to make these logs persistent.

Viewing log with journalctl

To view log

```
journalctl
```

To view full meta data about all entries

```
journalctl -o verbose
```

Live view of logs

```
journalctl -f
```

Filtering by Priority

You can filter the logs on basis of priority.

Syntax

```
journalctl -p priority
```

Example

In this example, we want to view only lines with error from the log

```
journalctl -p err
```

To view log entries only from the current boot

```
journalctl -b
```

To make logs persistent

```
$ sudo mkdir -p /var/log/journal
```

Then, restart journald to apply the change:

```
systemctl restart systemd-journald
```

Rsyslogd

Some logs are controlled by rsyslogd daemon. It is enhanced replacement of sysklogd. It offers high-performance, great security features, modular design and support for transportation via the TCP or UDP protocols. Every logged message contains at least a time and normally a program name field.

/etc/rsyslog.conf

The rsyslog.conf file is the main configuration file for the rsyslogd which logs system messages on the systems. This file specifies rules for logging rsyslogd. List of log files maintained by rsyslogd can be found in the rsyslog.conf configuration file. Log files are usually located in the /var/log/ directory.

Sample rsyslog.conf

```
etc]$ cat rsyslog.conf
# rsyslog v5 configuration file


# For more information see /usr/share/doc/rsyslog-
*/rsyslog_conf.html
# If you experience problems, see
http://www.rsyslog.com/doc/troubleshoot.html


*.info;mail.none;authpriv.none;cron.none
/var/log/messages


# The authpriv file has restricted access.
authpriv.*
/var/log/secure


# Log all the mail messages in one place.
mail.*                                              -
/var/log/maillog



# Log cron stuff
cron.*
/var/log/cron


# Everybody gets emergency messages
*.emerg                                             *


# Save news errors of level crit and higher in a special file.
```

```
uucp,news.crit
/var/log/spooler


# Save boot messages also to boot.log
local7.*
/var/log/boot.log
```

Log filtering with rsyslog.conf

There is too much logging happens in the system, if it is not filtered it become almost impossible to use these logs. To filter the logs, we use /etc/rsyslog.conf file. It has two parameter facility and priority separated with dot (.). Facility is name of process for which you want to log and priority specify level of log like debug, info, notice, warning, err, crit, alert, emerg or * for all type of messages you want to keep.

Example

```
# The authpriv file has restricted access.
authpriv.*
/var/log/secure


# Log all the mail messages in one place.
mail.*                                          -
/var/log/maillog
```

In the example where authpriv and mail is facility and priority is * which means all logs.

Rotating logs with logrotate

Logs needs rotation to avoid filling of file systems and make log more manageable. Once log file is rotated, it will be renamed with new file name. After certain time of rotation, older log files are deleted to save space.

logrotate package manages automatic rotation of log files according to configuration in **/etc/logrotate.conf** or otherwise specified with command option

Install

```
sudo apt install logrotate
```

To verify if logrotate installed successfully

```
logrotate
```

Some of the important configuration settings in /etc/logrotate.conf file are rotation-interval, log-file-size, permssions of files, missingok, rotation-count and compression.

Example

```
/var/log/dpkg.log {
    missingok
    monthly
    compress
    rotate 15
size 100M
}
```

In this example the log rotation utility rotate the logs for dpkg with following details :-

Missingok   ignore if logs are missing

Compress   compress the logs in gzip format

Monthly   log is rotated on monthly.

| rotate 15 | 15 days of logs would be kept. |

Size 100M   if logs become size of 100 megabytes it will be rotated otherwise it will be rotated at rotation interval i.e. monthly

Important logs

The main directory for logs is /var/log . Some of the important log files in this directory is worth mentioning

- wtmp
- utmp
- dmesg
- messages
- maillog
- spooler
- auth.log or secure
- yum.log
- boot.log

/var/log/wtmp and /var/run/utmp

The wtmp and utmp files keep track of users logging in and out of the system. These two files are binary files. You cannot directly read the contents of these files using text editor, cat or more command. You have to use specific command for that.

who command uses /var/run/utmp file to provide information about the users who are currently logged onto the system.

```
[root@centos2 log]# who
(unknown) :0             2018-10-02 05:34 (:0)
root      pts/0          2018-10-02 05:38 (192.168.131.1)
```

/var/log/wtmp file

This file maintains history of all logged in and logged out users. The **last** command uses this file to display listing of last logged in users.

```
[root@centos2 log]# last
root      pts/0         192.168.131.1      Tue Oct  2 05:38   still logged in
(unknown :0             :0                 Tue Oct  2 05:34   still logged in
reboot    system boot   3.10.0-514.el7.x   Tue Oct  2 05:33 - 05:47  (00:13)
root      pts/1         192.168.131.1      Mon Oct  1 13:23 - crash   (16:10)
root      pts/0         :0                 Mon Oct  1 13:21 - 13:35   (00:14)
root      :0            :0                 Mon Oct  1 13:20 - 13:35   (00:15)
----output truncated---
```

dmesg

dmesg obtains its data by reading the kernel ring buffer. A buffer is a portion of a computer's memory that is set aside as a temporary holding place for data that is being sent to or received from an external device. The messages are very important in terms of diagnosing purpose in case of device failure. Whenever there is hardware change happens most the time messages are logged here. If you are facing any problem you diagnose it using dmesg. dmesg tool is used to read dmesg file present in /var/log/ directory

```
[root@centos2 log]# dmesg |more
[    0.000000] Initializing cgroup subsys cpuset
[    0.000000] Initializing cgroup subsys cpu
[    0.000000] Initializing cgroup subsys cpuacct
[    0.000000] Linux version 3.10.0-514.el7.x86_64
(builder@kbuilder.dev.centos.org) (gcc version 4.8.5 20150623 (Red Hat 4.8.5-
11) (GCC) ) #1 SMP Tue Nov 22 16:42:41 U
TC 2016
[    0.000000] Command line: BOOT_IMAGE=/boot/vmlinuz-3.10.0-514.el7.x86_64
root=UUID=07547f5a-9e65-45a4-ab2d-2e8bb48bef3a ro crashkernel=auto rhgb quiet
LANG=en_US.UTF
---- output truncated---
```

Messages

General message are logged in this file. To view this file you can use text editor or any common tool for viewing text file like cat, less or more.

Example

```
[root@centos2 log]# cat messages
Oct  2 06:07:02 localhost rsyslogd: [origin software="rsyslogd"
swVersion="7.4.7" x-pid="1056" x-info="http://www.rsyslog.com"]
rsyslogd was HUPed
Oct  2 06:10:02 localhost systemd: Started Session 6 of user root.
Oct  2 06:10:02 localhost systemd: Starting Session 6 of user root.
Oct  2 06:20:01 localhost systemd: Started Session 7 of user root.
```

Maillog

This file logs the messages for mail server running on the server.

Example

```
[root@centos2 log]# cat maillog
Feb 25 16:26:24 centos1 postfix/postfix-script[1371]: starting the Postfix mail system
Feb 25 16:26:24 centos1 postfix/master[1379]: daemon started -- version 2.10.1,
configuration /etc/postfix
Feb 26 01:57:23 centos1 postfix/postfix-script[1980]: starting the Postfix mail system
Feb 26 01:57:24 centos1 postfix/master[2045]: daemon started -- version 2.10.1,
configuration /etc/postfix
Feb 26 23:43:36 centos1 postfix/postfix-script[1591]: starting the Postfix mail system
Feb 26 23:43:36 centos1 postfix/master[1641]: daemon started -- version 2.10.1,
configuration /etc/postfix
Feb 27 03:07:58 centos1 postfix/postfix-script[1670]: starting the Postfix mail system
Feb 27 03:07:58 centos1 postfix/master[1764]: daemon started -- version 2.10.1,
configuration /etc/postfix
Feb 27 18:13:22 centos1 postfix/postfix-script[1494]: starting the Postfix mail system
```

Spooler

Logs the spooler messages. Spooler is used by print queues to print.

secure

This file captures authenication logs. To check the log file you can use more or less command.

Yum.log

Yum command log file.

Example

```
# cat yum.log
Feb 27 00:16:36 Installed: amanda-libs-3.3.3-18.el7.x86_64
Feb 27 00:16:38 Installed: amanda-3.3.3-18.el7.x86_64
Feb 27 00:16:38 Installed: amanda-client-3.3.3-18.el7.x86_64
Feb 27 00:25:43 Erased: amanda-client-3.3.3-18.el7.x86_64
Feb 27 18:42:10 Installed: epel-release-7-9.noarch
Mar 04 10:19:19 Installed: tigervnc-server-1.8.0-
2.el7_4.x86_64
Mar 04 23:06:26 Installed: apr-1.4.8-3.el7_4.1.x86_64
Mar 04 23:06:26 Installed: apr-util-1.5.2-6.el7.x86_64
```

Boot.log

Contains information that are logged when the system boots.

```
[root@centos2 log]# cat boot.log
[  OK  ] Started Show Plymouth Boot Screen.
[  OK  ] Reached target Paths.
[  OK  ] Reached target Basic System.
[  OK  ] Found device VMware_Virtual_S 1.
        Starting File System Check on /dev/disk/by-
uuid/07547f5a-9e65-45a4-ab2d-2e8bb48bef3a...
[  OK  ] Started File System Check on /dev/disk/by-
uuid/07547f5a-9e65-45a4-ab2d-2e8bb48bef3a.
```

```
[  OK  ] Started dracut initqueue hook.
[  OK  ] Reached target Remote File Systems (Pre).
[  OK  ] Reached target Remote File Systems.
--- Output truncated -----------
```

These are the few log files we discussed, there are more files in the /var/log directory you can go through these files to know more about them.

## Chapter 28

Selinux

Selinux is Security Enhanced Linux. Selinux is kernel module that improves the Linux server security. This is one of the solution for implementation of Access Control in Linux.

Selinux implements MAC Mandatory Access Control. Selinux is set of security rules, which determine which process can access which file, directory or port etc. Selinux policy to access process, directory, and files is known as context. One goal of Selinux is to protect data and system. Selinux has three forms of access control:

1. Enforcing
2. Permissive
3. Disabled

Enforcing

Selinux denes access based on selinux policy rules.

Permissive

Selinux does not deny access but deniels are logged for the action that would have been denied if running in enforcing mode.

Disabled

Selinux is completely disabled

Check the installation

```
# rpm -qa | grep selinux
```

Install selinux

```
# yum install policycoreutils policycoreutils-python
```

Check current mode

```
# getenforce
```

Check the status

```
# sestatus
```

Main configuration file

/etc/selinux/config

To Change the mode

Edit /etc/Selinux/config configuration file and change selinux=enforcing to desired mode like selinux= permissive. After saving the file and reboot the server.

If you set the mode to permissive, you can check the log what Selinux is doing.

```
# cat /var/log/messages |grep -i selinux
```
Or
```
tail -f /var/log/audit/audit.log
```

Commands to display context

Description	Command
List process conext	ps auxZ
Display user context	ld –Z
Display files with context	ls -lZ
copy with context	cp -Z
mkdir with context	mkdir -Z

Tool to change context

```
# semanage
```

Show context

```
# semanage fcontext -1
```

Types

The main permission control method used in SELinux targeted policy to provide advanced process isolation is Type Enforcement. All files and processes are labeled as a type. Types define a SELinux domain for processes and a SELinux type for files

Example of Types are

httpd_sys_content_t

tmp_t

Add context

```
# semanage fcontext -a -t httpd_sys_content_t   /abc/zzz.txt
# ls -Z
-rw-r--r--. root root unconfined_u:object_r:samba_share_t:s0
zzz.txt
```

Set the context to default

```
# restorecon -v -t /abc/zzz.txt
```

Booleans

Booleans allow a part of Selinux policy to change at runtime without any knowledge of Selinux policy writing

List Booleans

```
# semanage boolean -l
```

Configure Booleans

In this example, we will allow ftp read and write access in user's home directory

1. list all

```
semanage boolean -l
```

2. list Booleans weather they are on/off

```
getsebool -a
```

3. Allow ftp read and write files in the user's home directory

```
setsebool -P ftp_home_dir on
```

4. Check

```
# getsebool ftp_home_dir
ftp_home_dir --> on
```

## Chapter 29

System Monitoring Tools

Continues monitoring is vital part of the system administration. System monitoring helps in properly provision resources for your projects. It also helps in fine tuning the server. Monitoring helps in avoiding the unnecessary down time due to resource bottleneck as proper monitoring you can add the required hardware before it leads to server crash or denial of service. Sometime monitoring helps in predicting the hardware failure for example you can use smart tools to predict hard disk failure.

Viewing system processes

ps

Display report of running process. It is a snapshot of the current processes at time of running command.

To see every process on the system and thire owner

```
ps aux
```

To list all related threads after each process

```
ps axms
```

Top

top command displays processor activity of Linux machine The top command displays list of running processes on the system It also displays additional information about current usage of CPU, memory and swap space.

```
# top
top - 21:59:05 up  5:58,  3 users,  load average: 0.16, 0.03, 0.01
Tasks: 188 total,   1 running, 187 sleeping,   0 stopped,   0 zombie
%Cpu(s):  0.0 us,  0.7 sy,  0.0 ni, 97.7 id,  1.0 wa, 0.3 hi,  0.3 si, 0.0 st
KiB Mem :  2045748 total,   168512 free,  1038120 used,   839116 buff/cache
KiB Swap:  2097148 total,  1906704 free,   190444 used.   891936 avail Mem


  PID USER      PR  NI    VIRT    RES    SHR S %CPU %MEM     TIME+ COMMAND
 1771 root      20   0  406112  10888   7084 S  0.3  0.5   0:30.40 vmtoolsd
 5854 root      20   0  156652   3960   3456 R  0.3  0.2   0:00.03 top
    1 root      20   0  215220   8316   5820 S  0.0  0.4   0:09.58 systemd
    2 root      20   0       0      0      0 S  0.0  0.0   0:00.03 kthreadd
    3 root      20   0       0      0      0 S  0.0  0.0   0:02.07
--- Output truncated ---
```

System Monitor Tool

System monitor tool is GUI tool for system monitoring. The Processes tab allows you to view, search for, change the priority of, and kill processes. In the menu Application > System tools > **System monitor**. Click **Processes** tab to view the list of running processes.

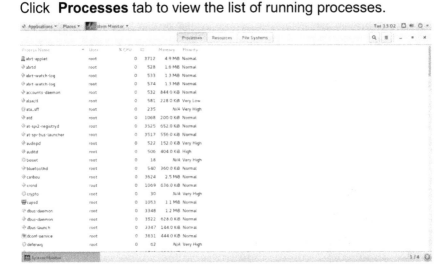

Click resources tab to check CPU, memory and Swap space utilization. It also shows network activities.

File system tab provide information about filesystem type, total size, available, used and percentage used.

Free

Free command provides information about system memory and swap space

```
~]# free
            total      used      free    shared  buff/cache   available
Mem:      2045748   1066888    135120     7596      843740      863048
Swap:     2097148    193704   1903444
```

To view memory in Megabytes

```
# free -m
```

lsblk

The blkid command displays information about available block devices which includes block device's major and minor number, size, type and mount point.

```
~]# lsblk -a
NAME          MAJ:MIN RM  SIZE RO TYPE MOUNTPOINT
sda            8:0     0   20G  0 disk
├─sda1         8:1     0    1G  0 part /boot
└─sda2         8:2     0 17.9G  0 part
  ├─cl-root 253:0      0 15.9G  0 lvm  /
  └─cl-swap 253:1      0    2G  0 lvm  [SWAP]
```

To get UUID of a block device

```
~]# blkid /dev/sda1
/dev/sda1: UUID="b4bd5914a11" TYPE="ext4" PARTUUID="f2f7d4-01"
```

Partx

The partx command display a list of disk partitions.

To display list of partition for a device

```
~]# partx -s /dev/sda
NR   START       END   SECTORS SIZE NAME UUID
 1    2048   2099199   2097152   1G       f2acf7d4-01
 2 2099200  41943039  39843840  19G       f2acf7d4-02
```

findmnt

The findmnt command allows you to list all mounted file systems

```
~]# findmnt
TARGET     SOURCE                 FSTYPE          OPTIONS
/          /dev/mapper/cl-root    xfs     rw,relatime,seclabel
├─/sys     sysfs       sysfs      rw,nosuid,nodev,noexec,r|
---Output truncated to fit in window-----
```

du

The du command allows you to display disk usage by files in a directory

```
~]# du
4          ./Templates
4          ./Music
4          ./.pki/nssdb
8          ./.pki
24         ./.gnupg
```

To display output in human readable format i.e. the size in KB and MB

```
~]# du -h
4.0K       ./Templates
4.0K       ./Music
4.0K       ./.pki/nssdb
8.0K       ./.pki
24K        ./.gnupg
```

Display summary

```
~]# du -sh
9.1M    .
```

df

The df command displays report of file system disk space usage.

To display the disk space usage by each file system

```
~]# df -h
Filesystem              Size  Used Avail Use% Mounted on
devtmpfs                476M     0  476M   0% /dev
tmpfs                   487M  336K  487M   1% /dev/shm
tmpfs                   487M  2.4M  485M   1% /run
--Output Truncated ---
```

www.ingramcontent.com/pod-product-compliance
Lightning Source LLC
Chambersburg PA
CBHW071116050326
40690CB00008B/1241